MEDITERRANEAN

Acknowledgements

I want to thank everyone first, but of course that is not possible! Thank you to Kyle Cathie, for thinking of me for this project, and for all the opportunities in food styling you have given me over the years for your Kyle Books, and now for writing this book. And to Sophie Allen for believing in the idea and then guiding me through it.

To John Kernick and Erika Oliveria for being such perfect partners to work with. John for his beautiful photography (and Rizwan for all the back-up in photography team) and Erika for art direction and design – for always having the bigger picture in mind with her design while we were shooting.

A big-big thanks to Gerri Noack for helping cook the majority of these recipes and working with me on the shoots.

And thank you to all the Greek Cypriot ladies in my life who all cook brilliantly and have taught me my whole life, although they now think I know more! I think not. Thank you. And of course, my grilling skills come from Dad; although he still does not let me light the grill when he is around!

And thanks to all my good friends who have shared many a Mediterranean meal with me, even when this book was not on the horizon, but the cuisine has always been my choice of food. I love it. I cannot have enough of roasted branzino, lemons and fennel!

Thank you to Alina Tierney, a registered nutritionist, for giving us a brilliant guide through the basic nutrition of the Mediterranean Diet that can be easily followed every day.

Susie

All recipe analyses are divided by the amount the recipe serves.

An Hachette UK Company
www.hachette.co.uk

First published in Great Britain in 2018
by Kyle Books, an imprint of Kyle Cathie Limited
Carmelite House, 50 Victoria Embankment
London EC4Y 0DZ
www.kylebooks.co.uk

Text © 2018 Susie Theodorou
Design and layout copyright © 2018 Kyle Cathie Ltd.
Photographs © 2018 John Kernick

Susie Theodorou is hereby identified as the author of this work in accordance with Section 77 of the Copyright, Designs and Patents Act 1988.

ISBN 978-085783-479-9

Project Editor: Sophie Allen
Editorial Assistant: Sarah Kyle
Creative Direction & Designer: Erika Oliveira
Design Production Assistant: Hollis Yungbliut
Photographer: John Kernick
Food and Prop Stylist: Susie Theodorou
Food Assistant: Gerri Noack
Production: Gemma John, Nic Jones and Lisa Pinnell

A Cataloguing in Publication record for this title is available from the British Library.

Colour reproduction by ALTA London
Printed and bound in China by C&C Offset Printing Co., Ltd.

10 9 8 7 6 5 4 3 2 1

MEDITERRANEAN

BY SUSIE THEODOROU

Photograpy by John Kernick

Kyle Books

Contents

The emphasis of the Mediterranean diet is fresh, simple and seasonal food – and using as few ingredients as possible. Recipes make the most of one's means – be it cheap cuts of meat (diets are low in beef, but make the most of sheep, goat and poultry) and pulses. And, of course, there is lots of fish and shellfish. Extra virgin olive oil is also key, containing many nutritional qualities that add to the overall healthiness of the diet.

The Mediterranean diet is what I grew up on. I have a Greek Cypriot background and, although I was born and raised in London, due to our lifestyle and diet, it was as if I grew up in a Mediterranean village. My mother and her five sisters (who were all working mothers), with the help of their mother (Yiayia), raised all eighteen cousins on a simple diet of freshly cooked meals. Some meals were quick mid-week dinners, others big extended family meals where we had hours at the social dinner table. All the food was freshly prepared – no microwaves, no frozen ready meals, no convenience whatsoever. The most 'convenient' foods in Mediterranean cooking are fresh, in-season fruit, vegetables, dairy, fish and meat. When food is in season, you need very little – extra virgin olive oil, lemon juice, salt and pepper – to prepare and serve with them.

As an adult and professional food stylist, I have travelled all over the Mediterranean. I have enjoyed spring, summer and autumn months, taking in the freshness of every season.

Food to the Mediterraneans is, in my understanding, about an appreciation of ingredients, enjoying the role of each ingredient, taking in the flavours of salty, bitter and sweet, and the textures of soft or crunchy. It's about being mindful of what you are eating. The Mediterranean diet can be high in carbohydrates (they do not count calories!), but they are careful of what and how much they eat. Mealtimes are also a time to sit down, relax with friends and family and enjoy what is in front of you, not stress about what has happened two hours earlier or what might happen in the future.

The outdoor lifestyle in the Mediterranean culture also helps to maintain a healthy life and in keeping stress to a low level. I remember a few years back, at the beginning of the Greek financial crisis, I asked locals that I was working with, 'Are you not stressed with all the problems right now?'. The answer, on more than a few occasions was, 'It's spring now, so it's new beginnings; we are going to enjoy the summer – sunshine, sea and food; and then, when we are at home in the winter, maybe we will worry!'. Ways to keep life less stressful are very important – it's not only the food that makes the Mediterranean diet healthy, but the state of mind as well.

Over the years, by cooking and entertaining for my friends, I have shown my love of the Mediterranean, even though I didn't really realise it at the time. This cookbook is a collection of Greek recipes I have enjoyed throughout my life (with a few tweaks here and there to make them a little easier and less time-consuming) and my interpretation of Italian and Spanish food, from my years of travelling and cooking with work. As a food stylist, I feel I am not an expert in any cuisine, but I very much fall back on my knowledge of Mediterranean food, and hope that I have made all the recipes in this book easy, accessible and delicious enough to be enjoyed by all of you.

The Mediterranean diet is a way of eating rather than a diet plan. It is an expression of the food cultures of the communities around the Mediterranean basin (Greece, Cyprus, Southern Italy, Spain, Morocco, Portugal and Croatia). It varies according to the particular area but, whether you are talking about the food of Italy or of Greece, you will inevitably be thinking about the abundance of seasonal vegetables, nuts, fruits and aromatic herbs, the bitter sweet taste of extra virgin olive oil, the freshly caught fish and tasty cheese, all possibly accompanied by a glass of red wine.

The history of the Mediterranean diet

The Mediterranean diet was 'found' in the olive-growing areas of Crete, Greece and Southern Italy in the late 1950s by Ancel Keys, an American physiologist who studied the influence of the diet on health. Following journeys in Southern Europe, he published the famous Seven Countries Studies paper where he showed that these Mediterranean countries had strikingly lower rates of coronary heart disease when compared with other study populations. Since then, the Mediterranean diet has been studied as a model of a healthy diet that has the ability to fight disease and increase your life expectancy.

According to Ancel Keys and his colleagues, the classical meals of the Mediterranean people always included a large amount of vegetables cooked or seasoned with olive oil and herbs. Fish was consumed in moderate amounts, while meat was an occasional treat. Cakes and sweet desserts were reserved for special occasions, while seasonal fruit was the typical dessert. Bread, cheese and wine (where allowed by the religion of the region) played central roles in their diet. Tree nuts and olives were also commonly consumed.

It is also worth mentioning that the people living in these communities that Keys observed were leading simple lives, working hard and relying almost entirely on local resources. Scarcity was the rule; abundance was the exception that led to festivities when people ate and drank much more indulgently.The Mediterranean diet is not just about food, but also a way to embrace and enjoy life. Many associate the word diet with food restriction. As a matter of fact, the word diet comes from the Ancient Greek word 'diaeta' meaning 'way of life', thus encompassing not only food habits but also the daily activities, culture and lifestyle that form these food habits.

What the Mediterranean diet consists of

When we talk about Mediterranean diet we are really talking about the traditional way of eating of the people living in Greece and Southern Italy before the 1960s. Most of the health benefits associated with the diet are based on this traditional diet and this is what we should aim for too. The Mediterranean climate is optimal for the cultivation of fruit and vegetables, some of which are native to the region, such as olive trees. The surrounding sea waters are a source of freshly caught fish. Animals, mainly goats and sheep, are free to graze in the local pastures.

The traditional Mediterranean diet is: seasonal vegetables and fruit, legumes and unprocessed cereals; moderate in fish and shellfish; olive oil is the core fat; meat and dairy consumption is low with the exception of some types of cheese that can keep well, which are often used for flavour; food preparation is simple and the flavour of meals is enhanced with aromatic herbs; people drink wine or tea with meals and water throughout the day; meals are structured and sociable.

The dietary features of the traditional Mediterranean diet include the following:

• Dishes are based on vegetables, legumes, fruit and extra virgin olive oil, accompanied by fruit and nuts as dessert or snacks: think of chickpeas with spinach, and broad beans with wild artichokes, doused in copious amounts of olive oil and finished off with walnuts and figs. These plant-based foods are high in vitamins and minerals, antioxidants and fibre, all of which are optimal for health and weight control. Vegetables and fruits are a great source of antioxidants and phytochemicals. Antioxidants are chemicals that protect our cells from the damaging effects of oxidation. Phytochemicals, such as polyphenols, are chemical compounds responsible for the great variety of colours of vegetables and fruit, and are thought to be responsible for the protective health benefits provided by these foods. As a general rule, the more intense the colour of a food the higher the phytochemical content.

• The type of olive oil used for all cooking and eating purposes was extra virgin. Extra virgin olive oil is a source of good healthy fats in the form of monounsaturated fatty acids (MUFAs).

• Garlic, onions, herbs and spices, generously used as condiments in the Mediterranean diet, contain large quantities of flavonoids, which not only have cardiovascular benefits but may also improve cognitive function. Oregano, which is added to many dishes, and seen growing wild in Mediterranean countries, is one of the richest sources of polyphenols among herbs. Other popular herbs include dill, mint, rosemary and wild fennel.

• Bread made from wholemeal flour and sourdough culture was consumed with most meals, including soups, cooked dishes, salads and even fruit. Due to the long fermentation process in its preparation, sourdough bread has a lower Glycaemic Index (GI) than most modern breads, meaning it has less impact on blood glucose levels. In addition, the sourdough fermentation improves the nutritional quality of bread. For example, it enhances the bioavailability of minerals as it causes degradation of anti-nutritive compounds usually found in unprocessed grains, such as phytic acid. Phytic acid binds to minerals making it harder for them to be absorbed from the gut. It also increases the degradation of gluten proteins and increases the digestibility of starches which makes it less likely to lead to gluten sensitivity. The starter culture used in the sourdough process can also beneficially influence your gut microbiota, thus improving your gut health.

• Rusks made from barley were also staple foods in Crete and they were softened with olive oil, further lowering the GI. Whole, unprocessed grains provide good amounts of dietary fibre and unique phytonutrients such as lignans and phenolic acids that complement those found in fruit and vegetables. They are also a good source of B vitamins and minerals, including magnesium and selenium.

• Some dairy, in the form of cheese and yogurt sourced mainly from sheep and goats, were regularly added to salads and vegetable stews. Goat's and sheep's milk contain A2 beta-casein, a protein found in breast milk, which some people seem to be able to tolerate better than the A1 beta-casein that is found in cow's milk.

• Meat was consumed in small amounts, as a source of flavour rather than the main ingredient and it usually came from small animals that roamed and grazed on pasture rather than being grain-fed. These pasture-fed animals provide omega-3 fatty acids to the diet. In addition, the cooking methods used to prepare the meats, which involved lower temperatures and higher moisture, with the frequent addition of herbs, prevents the formation of the damaging compounds that can occur in meat cooked at high temperatures.

• Depending on the proximity of the sea, fish and shellfish were consumed in high to moderate amounts and were preferred to meat. Seafood and fish are an excellent source of omega-3 fatty acids (EPA and DHA) which have anti-inflammatory and anti-clotting properties. In addition, a high intake of omega-3 fatty acids has been shown to increase levels of HDL ('good' cholesterol) and to reduce the risk of heart attack and stroke.

• Water was the main beverage but herbal teas, from sage for example, and various mountain herbs and coffee were also consumed, providing extra antioxidants and phenolic compounds. Wine, mainly red wine, was part of the traditional Mediterranean diet, if accepted by religious beliefs, but was generally only consumed with meals and in moderation. It is also worth mentioning that the wine was produced with local grapes and made using traditional methods, such as extracting the juice by mechanical processes or even pressing it with their feet, leaving it to ferment on its own without adding yeast and sugar to speed up the fermentation process, and preserving it without additional sulphites, which can be troublesome for some people.

The Med diet is more than just specific foods

The importance of the Mediterranean diet is not just in its specific foods and nutrients but also in the way in which the food is produced, cooked, eaten and shared. It is about sitting together at the table, socialising and communicating together; sharing values and transmitting traditions and rituals from generation to generation, strengthening the identity of communities that goes beyond the nutritional aspects of the Mediterranean diet.

For this reason, the Mediterranean diet was recognised by UNESCO in 2010 as an Intangible Heritage of Humanity, describing it as 'a set of skills, knowledge, practices and traditions ranging from landscape to the table. Eating together is the foundation of the cultural identity and continuity of communities throughout the Mediterranean basin. It is a moment of social exchange and communication, an affirmation and renewal of family, group or community identity'.

We live in a fast-paced time with different priorities. We might make efforts to include the foods specific to the Mediterranean diet, but we should also devote time and space for the cultural and lifestyle elements of the Mediterranean diet: spending time in the kitchen, preparing meals from fresh and seasonal foods; sitting around the table and sharing the food together with family and friends.

OLIVE OIL

For centuries olive oil has been treasured in the Mediterranean countries for its healing and nutritional properties. Olive oil is the hallmark of the Mediterranean diet and a whole section

The importance of the Mediterranean diet
is not just in its specific foods and nutrients
but also in the way in which the food is
produced, cooked, eaten and shared.

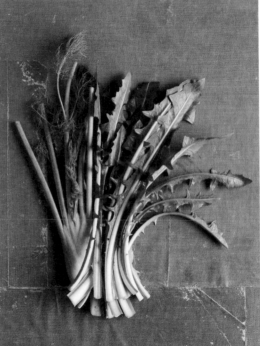

needs to be dedicated to it. It is estimated that olive oil provides some 85 percent of the fat content of this diet. This explains why the diet is low in saturated fats and cholesterol. The main type of fat in olive oil is monounsaturated fatty acids (MUFAs) which are considered healthy fats. High consumption of MUFAs is shown to lower the 'bad' LDL cholesterol and to raise the 'good' HDL cholesterol.

Olive oil is considered to be better than other vegetable oils due to the higher proportion of monounsaturated to polyunsaturated fatty acids which make it more resistant to the damaging effects of oxidation. As oil oxidises it becomes rancid and there are chemical changes within it that result in harmful compounds. In addition, oils derived from seeds, for example, sunflower oil, need to be refined for human consumption, which means that they lose the vast majority of nutritional compounds, turning them into just a mere source of fat.

Compared to other refined vegetable oils, olive oil contains many other non-fat components with great biological function, including vitamin E, carotenes, chlorophyll and a number of phenolic compounds.

For a long time it was thought that it was not safe to cook with olive oil at high temperatures, as it has a relatively low burning point, but recently it was shown that frying vegetables in extra virgin olive oil is safe and can actually increase their nutritional benefits, such as increasing their overall polyphenol content.

It was thought that the health benefits of olive oil were due to its high oleic fatty acids content. More recently, research indicates that it is actually compounds called polyphenols in olive oil that contribute to its benefits due to their strong antioxidant and anti-inflammatory properties.

The concentration of these phytochemicals in oils is influenced by the oil extraction procedure. Virgin and extra virgin oil contain the highest concentration of the polyphenols, while the lower quality olive oils are more deprived of these compounds. Extra virgin olive oil is obtained from the first pressing of the ripe fruit so has a high antioxidant content, while the refined olive oils lose their antioxidant and anti-inflammatory qualities during the physical-chemical procedures of the refinement.

So next time you are going to the shop, choose extra virgin olive oil in order to get the health benefits associated with olive oil, and avoid buying olive oil that is labelled 'pure olive oil' or just 'olive oil'. Some olive oils are blended with other vegetable oils to be used for frying at high temperatures, but these blends are stripped of the nutrients that are typically found in the extra virgin olive oil.

Health benefits of the Mediterranean diet
The traditional Mediterranean diet has been touted as one of the healthiest diets. This probably comes as no surprise considering its emphasis on a high consumption of plant-based foods and healthy fats which offer a plethora of nutrients that can help your body stay healthy.

Adhering to a traditional Mediterranean diet way of eating has been shown to improve your health in many ways:

Promotes heart health
Most of the attention of the scientific community on the

Mediterranean diet has focused on its effects on heart health. For the last 50 years, since Ancel Keys's first study on the Mediterranean diet, many studies have consistently demonstrated that adherence to the Mediterranean diet leads to protective cardiovascular effects. Two landmark studies, The Lyon Diet Heart Study (1999) (de Lorgeril et al, 1999) and the PREDIMED (Prevención con Dieta Mediterránea) study (2013) showed significant reduction in cardiovascular events and mortality in patients who followed a Mediterranean-style diet. Most amazingly, the PREDIMED study, which compared the Mediterranean diet to a low-fat diet, concluded after nearly five years, showing a highly significant 30 per cent reduction in major cardiovascular events. Not surprisingly, a systematic review published in 2009 (Mente et al.) ranked the diet as the most likely dietary model to provide protection against coronary heart disease.

Although the fat content of the Mediterranean diet is high, the cardioprotective effects are thought to be due to the high ratio of monounsaturated fat to saturated fat. In addition, the Mediterranean diet emphasises the consumption of natural, unprocessed foods that are loaded with vitamins, minerals and many other protective compounds that help your heart to stay healthy.

Prevention and management of diabetes

Most vegetables, fruit, legumes and whole cereals present in the Mediterranean diet tend to be low-glycaemic foods. These types of food cause a slower and lower rise in blood glucose levels than high glycaemic foods, such as white bread and pasta, and thus they are a better dietary choice for people living with diabetes whose bodies can't control their blood glucose levels as efficiently as a non-diabetic person.

The effects of the Mediterranean diet in the management of diabetes might not only be due to its effect on glycaemic control but also due to its fat composition. Mediterranean diets supplemented with extra virgin olive oil and nuts have been shown to be another factor in improving glucose metabolism, as they slow down the absorption of sugars from the gut into the bloodstream (Lasa et al., 2014).

The benefits of following a Mediterranean diet aren't just for those who already have diabetes, because it may also help in preventing developing this condition. Many prospective studies, in which individuals without diabetes were followed for many years to see if they developed the condition, showed that those who were adhering to the Mediterranean diet had overall reductions in risk ranging from 12 per cent to a staggering 83 per cent (Georgoulis et al., 2014).

Prevention and management of cancer

The overall incidence of cancer in Mediterranean countries is lower than in the majority of Western countries, including the UK. It has been estimated that up to 25 per cent of colorectal, 15 per cent of breast and 10 per cent of prostate, pancreas and endometrial cancers could be prevented by shifting to the traditional healthy Mediterranean diet (Trichopoulou et al., 2000).

More research is needed in this area but the protective effects of the Mediterranean diet could be due to the specific compounds that are found in vegetables, fruits, and nuts. For example, apigenin, which is found in artichokes, parsley and onion has been shown to have anti-tumour properties.

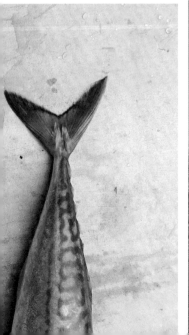

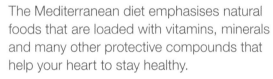

The Mediterranean diet emphasises natural foods that are loaded with vitamins, minerals and many other protective compounds that help your heart to stay healthy.

3ª-PM-1-4-03

Weight management

Although the traditional Mediterranean diet has a high fat content from olive oil and nuts, it was not found to cause people to gain weight. On the contrary, a few major randomised control studies found that people who followed the Mediterranean diet lost more weight than people that followed a low-fat diet (Shai et al., 2008).

Promotes longevity

Those that adhere to the principles of the traditional Mediterranean diet seem to have a greater rate of survival. A 2008 meta-analysis published in the British Medical Journal, showed that adherence to a Mediterranean diet led to a significant increase in life expectancy and a significant drop in the incidences of cardiovascular disease, cancer, Parkinson's disease and Alzheimer's disease (Sofi et al.).

The Mediterranean diet's emphasis on vegetables, fruits, wild herbs, nuts, sea food and extra virgin olive oil make it rich in antioxidants, phytonutrients, omega-3 fatty acids and monounsaturated fats, all of which are considered to be key factors in a longer and healthier life (Trichopoulou & Vasilopoulou, 2000).

Following the Mediterranean diet

Although our lifestyle and our relationship with food have changed since the 1960s, when the diet was first described, we are still encouraged to incorporate its features into our contemporary lifestyle. The latest Mediterranean diet pyramid (2010), as illustrated opposite, takes into consideration our contemporary lifestyle and it is a nice and easy illustration on how to follow this diet.

In summary:

• Aim for 1.5–2 litres of fluid per day in the form of water and herbal infusions.

• Every main meal should consist of three basic food groups: vegetables (2 servings or more; at least 1 serving to be raw), fruit (1–2 servings) and minimally refined cereals (1–2 servings). Include a variety of colours in order to ensure a wide variety of antioxidants and protective compounds.

• Every day you should aim for a handful of nuts, seeds and olives; infuse your meals with herbs, spices, garlic and onion, which help to keep your sodium intake low; and 1–2 servings of dairy products in the form of cheese and yogurt.

• Extra virgin olive oil should be the principal source of fat. It can be used for both cooking and dressings.

• In accordance with religious and social beliefs, wine (1 glass per day for women and 2 glasses per day for men, as a generic reference) is also present in the pyramid opposite.

• On a weekly basis, include fish (2 or more servings, 1 of which to be oily fish), white meat (2 servings) and eggs (2–4 servings). Consumption of red meat (less than 2 servings) and processed meats (less than 1 serving) should be small in both quantity and frequency. Legumes (more than 2 servings) are a good source of plant protein and thus a good meat alternative. Potatoes should be consumed in moderation (3 or fewer servings) and freshly made rather than pre-packed.

• Occasionally you can have sweets but in small amounts and for special occasions.

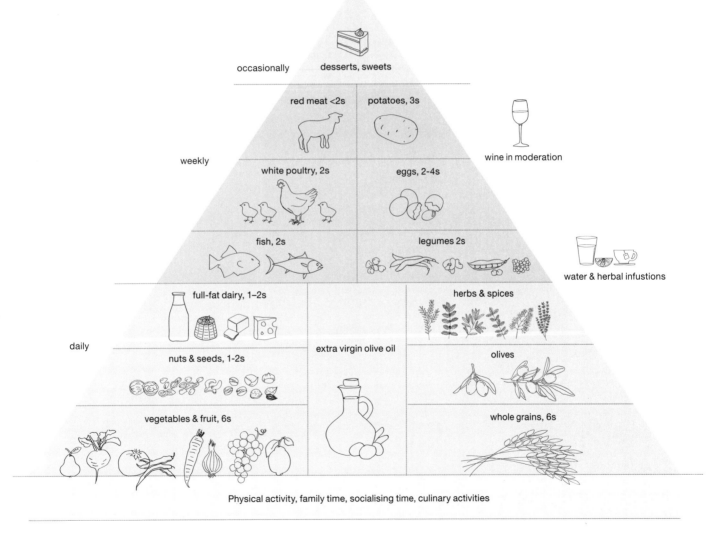

occasionally — desserts, sweets

weekly

red meat <2s — potatoes, 3s

white poultry, 2s — eggs, 2-4s

fish, 2s — legumes 2s

wine in moderation

water & herbal infustions

daily

full-fat dairy, 1–2s — herbs & spices

nuts & seeds, 1-2s — extra virgin olive oil — olives

vegetables & fruit, 6s — whole grains, 6s

Physical activity, family time, socialising time, culinary activities

s = serving Adapted from Bach-Faig et al. (2011). Mediterranean diet pyramid today. Science and cultural updates. Public Health Nutrition. 14(12A): 2274-84.

Olive oil is the hallmark of the Mediterranean diet and, for centuries, it has been treasured in the Mediterranean for its healing and nutritional properties.

CLEVER COOK – NOT A LAZY COOK

Mediterranean food is, above all else, about the ingredients. The quality of the locally grown, seasonal produce from the region, whether it's sun-ripened tomatoes or acorn-fed Iberico ham, is so full of flavour that it's every time-poor cook's dream. It needs no fussy preparation or fancy sauces and is best served very simply, on a board or a platter, together with two or three other ingredients that provide contrasting, complementary flavours and textures to ensure the distinctive tastes really shine through.

The ingredient pairings and combinations that follow are therefore not any kind of super-new innovation, and in many cases they hardly qualify as a recipe at all. However, they're a reminder of just how good a few basic, quality ingredients can be.

The recipes in this chapter can stand alone, making a light lunch or snack or appetiser; or they can be served as part of a menu of small, shared plates. As you go through, you will notice a pattern to my tastes as each one includes a little saltiness, coming from a smoked meat, a cheese or a preserved fish, which is then complemented with a little sweetness, often derived from fruit, and nearly always finished off with peppery extra virgin olive oil.

WHITE BEAN PURÉE

For convenience, you can use canned beans to make this purée. However, even though they are cooked, drain and simmer them in 300ml water with the lemon, onion and parsley for 20 minutes before you purée them, as otherwise the dip will lack flavour.

250g dried cannellini beans, soaked overnight and drained
½ lemon, roughly chopped
½ onion, peeled and quartered
2–3 flat-leaf parsley sprigs
50ml extra virgin olive oil
sea salt and freshly cracked black pepper
a topping of your choice (see page 29)
flatbread, to serve

Place the beans in a medium-large pot with a lid and cover with plenty of water, at least 10cm above the beans. Bring to the boil, skimming the surface of any white foam.

Reduce to a simmer, add the lemon, onion and parsley, partially cover with the lid and simmer for 1½ hours, until the beans are very tender. Half-way through, season with a little salt and pepper.

Drain the beans, reserving the liquid, lemon and onion, discard the parsley, and place in a food-processor or blender. Purée the beans with the reserved chopped lemon and onion until smooth, adding the oil a little at a time, and a little of the reserved cooking liquid if required. Taste and adjust the seasoning if necessary, then spread over a large plate, scatter with a topping and serve with flatbread.

SERVES 4 281 calories, 29.7g carbs, 13.4g fat, 1.9g sat fat, 12.3g protein

HUMMUS

For me, shop-bought hummus has too much flavour, especially too much garlic. I grew up eating hummus that was made with no garlic, roasted or otherwise, and I love the very simple but genius pairing of chickpeas with sesame tahini. As with the White Bean Purée, you can speed up the recipe by using drained canned chickpeas, and again I recommend you cook them with the flavourings for 20 minutes.

225g dried chickpeas, soaked overnight and drained
½ onion, sliced
2 flat-leaf parsley sprigs
3 tablespoons tahini paste
juice of 1 lemon
sea salt and freshly cracked black pepper
a topping of your choice (see page 29)
flatbread, to serve

Place the chickpeas in a medium-large pot with a lid and cover with plenty of water, at least 10cm above the chickpeas. Bring to the boil, skimming the surface of any white foam.

Reduce to a simmer, add the onion and parsley, partially cover with the lid and simmer for 1½ hours, until the chickpeas are very tender.

Drain the chickpeas, reserving the liquid and onion and discarding the parsley, and place in a food-processor or blender.

Place the tahini in a small bowl and whisk with 75ml of the reserved cooking liquid until smooth. Add the lemon juice and whisk again.

Add the tahini and lemon mixture to the chickpeas and purée until smooth, adding a little extra cooking liquid if necessary. Season to taste with salt and pepper, then spread over a large plate, scatter with a topping and serve with flatbread.

SERVES 4 247 calories, 29.5g carbs, 8.9g fat, 1.1g sat fat, 14g protein

Hummus with Preserved Lemon, Cucumber and Sesame

Fava Bean Dip with Olives, Tomatoes and Rosemary

FAVA BEAN DIP

The Greeks and southern Italians serve this fava bean purée as a dip or as a simple sauce with meats and fish.

225g craked fava (dried broad) beans, washed and drained
900ml water
1 medium onion, roughly chopped
pinch of sea salt flakes
75ml extra virgin olive oil, plus extra for drizzling
juice of 1 lemon
a topping of your choice (see right)
flatbread, to serve

Place the fava beans in a large sauté pan with a lid, cover with the water and bring to the boil, skimming the surface of any white foam.

Reduce to a simmer, add the chopped onion, cover with the lid and cook for 30 minutes.

Remove the lid, stir the beans and season with salt. Continue to cook for 15 minutes, uncovered, until most of the liquid evaporates and the beans are very soft. Allow to cool slightly.

Transfer the beans to a food-processor or blender. Add the olive oil and lemon juice little by little and process until super smooth. Taste, add extra lemon juice and salt if necessary, then spread over a large plate, scatter with one of the toppings and serve with flatbread.

SERVES 4 319 calories, 21.3g carbs, 19.9g fat, 2.8g sat fat, 15g protein

Toppings

OLIVES, TOMATOES AND ROSEMARY

Heat a large cast-iron pan until very hot. Add 300g cherry tomatoes and cook until they char, about 2–3 minutes, then add 75g Kalamata olives, pitted, and 3 tablespoons extra virgin olive oil. Stir once, then add 2 large sprigs of rosemary, broken into small sprigs and season. Cook for another minute, then stir in 2 tablespoons red wine vinegar and swirl the pan to incorporate all flavours. Spoon over the purée of your choice and serve.

SERVES 4 112 calories, 2.7g carbs, 10.7g fat, 1.5g sat fat, 1g protein

PRESERVED LEMON, CUCUMBER AND SESAME

Chop 1 preserved lemon (about 75g), including the flesh as well as the rind, and sprinkle over a plate of hummus or bean purée. Top with 100g finely sliced cucumber, a sprinkling of sea salt and a drizzle of extra virgin olive oil (about 3 tablespoons). Finally, scatter with 2 tablespoons toasted sesame seeds and serve.

SERVES 4 119 calories, 1g carbs, 11.9g fat, 1.8g sat fat, 1.5g protein

QUICK PICKLED RED ONIONS

In a small bowl, mix 2 tablespoons red wine vinegar with a pinch each of salt and sugar; stir to dissolve. Add 1 small red onion or 2 shallots, thinly sliced on a mandolin, toss to mix and set aside for 10 minutes. Drain the onions, then scatter all over the hummus or bean purée, and drizzle with 3 tablespoons extra virgin olive oil to serve.

SERVES 4 79 calories, 0.8g carbs, 8.2g fat, 1.1g sat fat, 0.2g protein

GEM LETTUCE SALAD

Break up 1 small head of Little Gem lettuce into individual leaves and tear any large ones in half or in to thirds. Place in a bowl and toss with 4 tablespoons extra virgin olive oil, 3 anchovies in oil, drained and chopped, and 2 tablespoons red wine vinegar. Season to taste. Spoon over the bean hummus or purée to serve.

SERVES 4 107 calories, 0.4g carbs, 11.2g fat, 1.6g sat fat, 0.9g protein

Prosciutto crudo – this is an Italian dry-cured ham made from the hind leg of a pig or wild boar that is rubbed with salt and spices and often aged 10–12 months. Traditionally, they were made in the winter, to be served 1–2 years later. It is most often served uncooked, thinly sliced and with an aperitif or as part of an antipasti platter. It has a salty, gamey taste that goes perfectly with drinks. Each prosciutto crudo is very local, and traditional to its region.

Prosciutto cotto – is ham that has been cooked. It is the kind you often find in a cheese and ham sandwich.

Culatello – this is another Italian regional ham, often from Zibello, south of Parma, very close to the Po River (it's all about the winds over the river and so on). It is very expensive as you can only use the muscular part of each hind leg of the pig.

Italian speck – not to be confused with the German bacon type of ham, the Italian speck is very similar to prosciutto but the meat has been cured first with spices and then lightly smoked.

Iberico ham – the Spanish and Portuguese version of dry-cured ham. 'Iberico' refers to the breed of black pigs, traditionally fed on acorns. There are four labels to choose from – black, red, green and white, with black being the most expensive – the length of the ageing process is longer. The deeper the colour and more marbling you see, the better the ham as the richer it will taste. The ham is hand-cut and served with drinks.

Serrano ham – a Spanish dry-cured ham, 'serrano' means ham from the Sierra mountain range where the common breed are white pigs. It is not as expensive or quite as prestigious as the Iberico ham; still, it is delicious, served thinly sliced.

Pancetta – we know pancetta as Italian bacon, a salt-cured pork belly made with black peppercorns and other spices. Often, you find it cubed and used in pasta sauces and so on. In Italy, it is common to serve it thinly sliced, as part of an antipasti meat selection

Lountza – this is cured and lightly smoked meat made from pork tenderloin. It is one of the most popular delicacies of Cypriot cuisine, where it is brined, marinated in red wine and then dried and smoked. Serve thinly sliced.

Fruit with Ham

ROASTED FIGS WITH PROSCIUTTO

Preheat the oven to 200°C/400°F/gas mark 6. Wrap a thin slice of cured prosciutto (of your choice) around a sweet ripe fig and place on a baking tray. Drizzle lightly with extra virgin olive oil, season with a pinch of sea salt and grind of black pepper. Roast in the oven for 10 minutes. Transfer to a serving platter, drizzle with a little more oil and sprinkle with Calabrian chilli flakes. Serve with a small dressed salad of rocket or shredded radicchio leaves.

SERVES 1 84 calories, 5.2g carbs, 5.1g fat, 1.1g sat fat, 4.8g protein

PROSCIUTTO AND MELON

Once, when I was in Verona, I was served thinly sliced prosciutto on wax paper, with wedges of fragrant orange-fleshed melon, all drizzled with extra virgin olive oil. It tasted so good and I've recreated the dish many times (using the waxed paper too!). I like to use sweet cantaloupe and charentais melons.

SERVES 1 109 calories, 6.8g carbs, 5.4g fat, 1.5g sat fat, 8.7g protein

PROSCIUTTO, WHITE PEACHES AND ROCKET

I just love this flavour combination; the fresh sweetness of a white peach with the zingy, peppery rocket and salty prosciutto. Always drizzle with a little extra virgin olive oil and season with freshly cracked black pepper and, if you like, you can grill the peaches first and sprinkle with Calabrian chilli flakes before you serve.

SERVES 1 112 calories, 5.3g carbs, 5.6g fat, 1.5g sat fat, 10.7g protein

Roasted Figs with Prosciutto

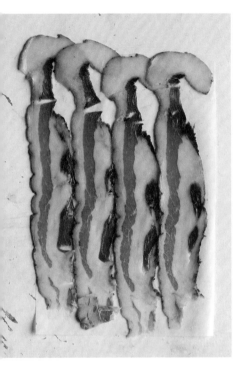

Left: pancetta; Bottom left: black mission figs; above: Cantaloupe melon; below: prosciutto crudo; top right: olive tree; right: prosciutto cotto

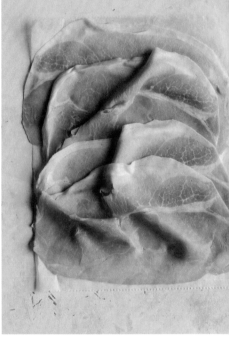

The prestigiuous prosciutto di san Danielle

TUNA, SARDINES AND MACKEREL

Even though fresh fish is prominent in a Mediterranean diet, canned tuna, sardines, mackerel and anchovies are all common in the region and are often accompanied with beans to provide a nutritious protein-rich meal. Be discerning about fishing and preserving methods and go for quality. Ideally, choose line- or pole-caught tuna as these fishing methods are dolphin-safe. For tuna and anchovies, Ortiz is my favourite brand, especially the tuna belly – it is not cheap, but worth splashing out on every now and again. And remember some of these canned fish can be bought in a jar too.

Mackerel salad Drain the mackerel and flake onto a flat plate. Drizzle with lemon juice and extra virgin olive oil and scatter with capers. Serve with crispbread.

Sardines and cucumber Place the sardines on a serving plate and top with finely sliced cucumber. Drizzle with extra virgin olive oil, scatter with toasted sesame seeds and serve.

Tuna with black olives and tomatoes Flake tuna onto a plate. Mix chopped tomatoes with pitted black olives and finely chopped flat-leaf parsley. Spoon over the tuna, drizzle with lemon juice and extra virgin olive oil. Season to taste.

Sardines on toast Place the sardines on toast and scatter with chopped celery leaves, a pinch of dried chillies and a sprinkle of sea salt and freshly cracked black pepper.

Tonnato sauce In a food-processor, whizz up 1 x 190g can of tuna in oil, drained, with 2 anchovy fillets and 2 tablespoons capers. Add 4 heaped tablespoons mayonnaise, juice of ½ lemon and 2 tablespoons extra virgin olive oil. Taste, and season with a pinch of dried chillies, salt and black pepper. Serve as a dip or with pasta.

ANCHOVIES

Anchovies, in particular, are incredibly versatile and used as an ingredient to flavour meats (especially good with lamb), enrich salad dressings, make a simple pasta sauce, or to add extra salty flavour to vegetables, such as broccoli or cauliflower, or used in dressings for a tomato-based salad. To use salt-cured anchovies: wash, split open with a small paring knife and with your fingers, peel away the central bone and discard, and then use the two fillets. Don't worry if you do not use all the anchovies, simply cover the can with clingfilm, refrigerate and use as required.

Tomatoes on toast Slice a heritage tomato, place on a piece of bread, add an anchovy fillet and a drizzle of extra virgin olive oil.

Stuffed green olives Stuff a big green olive with an anchovy fillet. If it's too difficult to stuff, wrap the anchovy around the olive and skewer with a cocktail stick to secure.

Watermelon Wrap an anchovy fillet around a square of chilled watermelon. Secure with a cocktail stick.

Boiled eggs Wrap an anchovy fillet around half a soft-boiled egg. Secure with a cocktail stick.

Pear Serve an anchovy fillet with a wafer-thin slice of pear.

Pasta Heat 4 tablespoons extra virgin olive oil in a small frying pan. Add 1 x 50g can anchovies, drained, and break up with a fork while they sizzle. Add a sprinkling of chilli flakes, then stir and add 225g cooked spaghetti, together with a little pasta cooking water, if needed. Drizzle with extra virgin olive oil, toss with crispy breadcrumbs and serve.

Clockwise from top left: tuna belly in oil (Ortiz), sardines in tomato sauce, mackerel fillets in oil, tuna in olive oil, anchovies in oil

Homemade Boquerones

BOQUERONES

Boquerones are anchovies that have been cured in salt, then soaked in vinegar. They are sold in a light vinegar oil and are not canned but vacuum-sealed and can be found in the fridge section of the supermarket or deli. Recently, when I was working in Madrid, I needed a simple quick bite one evening as I had a touch of jet-lag to contend with. I ordered a plate of boquerones and oh how I enjoyed them all to myself! They were served swimming in a peppery extra virgin olive oil, with a few big green olives and small crunchy pieces of cracker. And of course a glass of ice-cold rosé – perfection.

Boquerones fritos Toss the boquerones with flour and salt and freshly cracked black pepper until evenly coated. Pour olive oil into a frying pan, at least 1.5cm deep, and shallow-fry the boquerones until golden. Dress with finely chopped flat-leaf parsley, lemon zest and chilli flakes and serve hot with sea salt flakes and wedges of lemon.

HOMEMADE BOQUERONES

It's hard to give exact quantities but as it does take 2–3 days to make these, you might as well make at least a kilo so that you have enough to snack on for at least 2 weeks. You can also make these with small sardines.

1kg fresh anchovies, cleaned and butterflied with bones
and head removed
sea salt flakes
enough vinegar or lemon juice to cover for soaking (red
wine, white wine or sherry vinegar)
4 tablespoons chopped flat-leaf parsley
1 tablespoon Calabrian chilli flakes (optional)
2 garlic cloves, thinly sliced (optional)
extra virgin olive oil

Wash the anchovies and pat dry. Sprinkle with salt flakes and then close up each butterflied fillet.

Spread a layer of salt flakes over the base of a non-metallic dish and layer the anchovies on top. Cover and set aside for 3 hours.

Wash the fish and pat dry, then layer again in a clean, deep-sided non-metallic dish and pour over the vinegar or lemon juice. Cover and refrigerate for 24 hours.

Drain and transfer the anchovies to a clean re-sealable container. Add the parsley, chilli flakes and/or garlic, then top with extra virgin olive oil, submerging them completely. Shake the container a little to allow any air bubbles to rise to the surface and disappear. Cover and refrigerate for at least 4 hours or until required. Serve as many as are needed, then refrigerate the remainder.

PER 100G 184 calories, 0.1g carbs, 12.2g fat, 2.2g sat fat, 16.8g protein

ALL ABOUT ROE

Fish roe, in all its many varieties, is found all through Mediterranean cooking. The Greeks have *tarama* (cod's roe, often smoked or fresh), the Italians *bottarga* (the roe from grey mullet or blue fin tuna that have been salt-cured and dried) and the Spaniards have *mojama* (a cured and dried tuna loin).

The Greeks make a dip known as taramasalata in the outside world, but in Greece and Eastern Mediterrean countries, it's known as Tarama. It's not really pink, that's the food colouring added to the product sold in supermarkets. The tarama can be made into a dip, but more recently it is popping up as a simple crème/sauce for vegetables and seafood appetisers. It's in season in spring and early summer.

Bottarga is not cheap to buy, but not too expensive either, with a very long shelf-life. *Bottarga di muggine* is from Sardinia, *bottarga di tonno* originated in Sicily and some would also say Calabria. Once cured and aged, it is completely covered with a wax seal (often beeswax). To use, remove only as much of the wax or seal to reveal what you will need, grate (using a microplane) or slice with a mandolin. To keep the remainder, simply wrap first in parchment paper, then foil, then pop in the fridge.

TARAMA(salata)

I like the flavour of this dip to be of pure smoked cod's roe, but you can add finely grated onion and/or garlic if you like (use a microplane to do this). Serve as a dip as part of a mezze menu or follow some of the simple serving ideas below.

300g white bread, crusts removed
200g smoked cod's roe
juice of 1 lemon
200ml extra virgin olive oil
pinch of sea salt

Place the bread in a large bowl and pour over enough warm water to cover. Once it starts to feel soft, squeeze the water out with your hands, discard the water, and place the bread in a food-processor or blender.

Split the skin from the roe and add to the food-processor. Initially, add half the lemon juice and start to pulse, then add the olive oil in a steady stream until the mixture forms a thick paste. Taste, add a little extra lemon juice if needed and a pinch of salt. If you feel the mixture is too thick, add 1–2 tablespoons of warm water to the mixture and process once more. It should now be super smooth.

PER 100G 474 calories, 15g carbs, 41.3g fat, 6g sat fat, 11.4g protein

Simple ways to serve tarama

With grilled fish Spread 2 tablespoons of tarama on a serving plate and top with grilled white fish, such as cod, halibut or swordfish. Drizzle with extra virgin olive oil and finish with radish slices or rocket.

On toast Cut thick slices of bread into fingers and toast. Spread with a little tarama and top with sliced cucumber and radishes. Finish with freshly cracked black pepper and extra virgin olive oil.

With radishes Spread the tarama on a serving plate, top with freshly shaved radishes, drizzle with extra virgin olive oil and season with sea salt and freshly cracked black pepper.

Tarama on Toast

Bottarga with Olive-Oil Fried Egg

BOTTARGA

Simply grate it using a microplane over pasta dressed with a little olive oil, or shave over crostini or a simple fried egg, and the transformation is unbelievable.

3 simple ways to serve bottarga

QUICK LINGUINE WITH BOTTARGA

Use the grey mullet variety, what the Italians call *bottarga di muggine*.

50g bottarga, grated with a microplane
juice of 1 lemon
350g squid ink spaghetti or linguine (or see page 67 for
   homemade pasta)
6 tablespoons extra virgin olive oil
½–1 teaspoon chilli flakes
sea salt and freshly cracked black pepper
extra bottarga or extra virgin olive oil, to serve

In a small bowl, whisk the grated bottarga with the lemon juice.

Cook the pasta in a large pot of boiling salted water for 8–10 minutes until al dente. Drain, reserving about 150ml of the pasta water.

Add a little of the reserved water to the bowl of bottarga and whisk to mix well. Heat the oil in a pan, add the chilli flakes and cook for 1 minute. Return the pasta to the hot pan and toss with the bottarga mixture, adding a little more of the reserved water, if needed. Taste and season, if necessary.

Divide the pasta between individual serving plates and sprinkle with bottarga and extra virgin olive oil to serve.

SERVES 4 458 calories, 58.4g carbs, 20.6g fat, 3.3g sat fat, 13.5g protein

OLIVE-OIL FRIED EGG

This recipe is for a picture-perfect fried egg (of course it's the food stylist in me)! A non-stick frying pan is essential. Freshly grated Parmesan is a good substitute for bottarga, if you can't find it.

4–6 asparagus spears
1 egg
2 tablespoons extra virgin olive oil
bottarga di tonno, grated with a microplane, to serve

For the asparagus, blanch in boiling water for 2 minutes, drain and cool to just warm. Place a non-stick frying pan over a medium heat. First break the egg white into the hot pan so that it sets into a perfect-ish round. Now drop the yolk in the middle. Drizzle the oil around the edge of the white and cook slowly, spooning the oil over the white as it fries.

Once the egg yolk is set to your liking, lift it out with a flat spatula and place on a serving plate. Add the cooked asparagus, sprinkle with grated bottarga di tonno to serve.

SERVES 1 218 calories, 0.8g carbs, 20.1g fat, 3.4g sat fat, 8.4g protein

IN-SEASON TENDER VEGETABLES

The simplest way to serve young, crisp vegetables is with a sprinkling of something – bottarga is a good alternative to sea salt flakes! Adjust servings for one to a crowd!

fresh young peppery radishes and/or sweet asparagus
extra virgin olive oil
finely grated bottargo di tonno

Prepare the radishes by washing and keep the leaves intact. For asparagus, blanch in boiling water for 2 minutes, drain and cool to just warm. Place the peppery extra virgin olive oil in a small bowl and the finely grated bottargo in another small bowl and arrange on the table. Serve the vegetables on a platter with the bowls within easy reach for dipping and sprinkling.

SERVES 1 218 calories, 0.8g carbs, 20.1g fat, 3.4g sat fat, 8.4g protein

EVERYONE'S FAVOURITE FRESH CHEESE

Originally, all these delicious Mediterranean cheeses were made with either goat's, sheep's or buffalo milk. Now, because of high market demand, cow's milk often creeps into the production so keep an eye on the label and choose the former rather than the latter – from a cooking point of view, for authenticity of flavour and for nutritional purposes (less people are intolerant of goat's and sheep's milk).

Feta is a brined curd white cheese made from sheep's milk or a mixture of sheep's and goat's milk. Look for traditional feta made in Greece or Bulgaria as, if it's made in the UK or the States, it is most likely to be made from cow's milk and is often saltier than usual.

Mozzarella and burrata originate from southern Italy and are soft white creamy cheeses traditionally made with buffalo milk. Mozzarella is the classic pizza topping and tricolore salad ingredient and burrata is very popular these days for its mozzarella outer wall and creamy curd filling. They are often sold as one large 150g ball and should be served at room temperature. With these two cheeses, when they are made with buffalo milk, you will notice an appealing tang, slightly salty taste to the cheese. When made with cow's milk, it's a clean, almost bland milk taste.

Halloumi is a semi-hard cheese made from goat's and sheep's milk that is always salty as it's preserved in brine. It is extremely versatile and can be crumbly or squeaky soft, served cooked or uncooked, and sliced or grated. One of my favourite ways is to grill the halloumi on the barbecue and serve warm in toasted pitta bread with a little rocket or mint – it's perfect 'standing around the barbecue food' while waiting for the souvlaki to cook!

Ricotta crosses over many Mediterranean countries. However, it originates in Italy and is made from the whey of goat's or sheep's milk left over from the production of other cheeses. It is soft and creamy in texture and has a very fresh, tangy flavour when made with goat's or sheep's milk. When buying ricotta, look for the type that is either sold in a packet with an inner-draining container, where you can turn the cheese out from any juices, or look for a large cake/round shape, that is sold in large sliced pieces. Avoid ricotta stuffed in a plastic container with no draining as it's too gluey, sticky and dense rather than a traditional light texture. For me, ricotta is a perfect breakfast cheese too, served with fresh fruit and honey. I also love to eat it with chestnut honey and soft, ciabatta-style bread.

All the recipes that follow are quick snacks, shared appetisers or light meal suggestions. All the toppings and the cheeses can be swapped around to suit your tastes. For optimum flavour, ensure the cheese and toppings start at room temperature, and also allow standing time for the flavours to come together. If using feta or halloumi, refrain from seasoning the topping until it is plated with the cheese and go carefully due to the saltiness of the cheese.

Opposite page top from left: Bulgarian feta; Greek feta; domestic cow's milk feta. Middle from left: torn burrata; tied buffalo burrata; halloumi cheese. Bottom from left: Buffalo mozzarella; small mozzarella balls; fresh ricotta

SWEET PEAS AND TARRAGON

75g sugar snap peas, trimmed and blanched
50g fresh podded peas
1 tablespoon tarragon leaves
juice of ½ lemon
4 tablespoons extra virgin olive oil
pinch of sea salt
1 x 150g burrata

Slice the sugar snap peas on the bias and place in a
bowl with the uncooked peas, tarragon, lemon juice and
olive oil. Mix together and season with salt to taste.

Partially split open the burrata into four pieces on a
serving plate and spoon over the sugar snap and pea
mixture. Leave to stand for 10 minutes, then serve.

SERVES 4 200 calories, 2.5g carbs, 18.2g fat, 6.1g sat fat, 6.6g protein

HERITAGE TOMATO AND OREGANO

1 large heritage tomato of your choice
2 tablespoons oregano leaves, roughly chopped
  or torn
4 tablespoons extra virgin olive oil
2 tablespoons red wine vinegar
150g feta, broken into 2–3 pieces
sea salt and freshly cracked black pepper

Slice the tomato into large chunks and place in a bowl
with the oregano, oil and vinegar. Stir gently, season to
taste and leave to stand for 10 minutes.

Place the feta on a serving plate, spoon over the tomato
salad and serve.

SERVES 4 200 calories, 1.7g carbs, 18.6g fat, 6.7g sat fat, 6.1g protein

COURGETTE AND MINT

75g small yellow, green or stripy courgette
4 tablespoons extra virgin olive oil
6–8 mint leaves
1 x 150g buffalo mozzarella ball
sea salt flakes and freshly cracked black pepper
1–2 courgette flowers, torn, to serve (optional)

Cook the courgette whole in a pan of boiling salted water for 1 minute. Drain and thinly slice while still warm.

Place the warm courgette in a bowl, mix in the oil and mint and season to taste.

Partially split open the mozzarella on a serving plate. Spoon over the courgette mixture and leave to stand for 10 minutes. Scatter with courgette flowers to serve.

SERVES 4 199 calories, 0.4g carbs, 18.7g fat, 6.7g sat fat, 7.4g protein

ESCAROLE AND CHILLI FLAKES

3 tablespoons extra virgin olive oil
100g escarole or dandelion leaves, washed and dried
½ teaspoon Calabrian chilli flakes
juice of ½ lemon
1 x 150g burrata
sea salt and freshly cracked black pepper

Heat the oil in a frying pan and add the escarole or dandelion leaves and chilli flakes. As soon as the leaves wilt, drain and place on a serving plate. Add the lemon juice to the pan juices and season with salt and pepper.

Partially split open the burrata into four pieces on the escarole or dandelion leaves, spoon over the oil juices and leave to stand for 5 minutes. Serve warm.

SERVES 4 161 calories, 0.4g carbs, 15.3g fat, 5.7g sat fat, 5.5g protein

PAN-FRIED BLACK OLIVES AND ROSEMARY

4 tablespoons extra virgin olive oil
75g oil-cured black olives, pitted
½ teaspoon Calabrian chilli flakes
2 small rosemary sprigs, de-stalked
2 tablespoons red wine vinegar
150g fresh ricotta, drained

Heat the oil in a small frying pan and add the olives and chilli flakes. Cook over a gentle heat for about 2 minutes until the olives start to sizzle and plump up. Add the rosemary and cook for a further minute, remove from the heat and stir in the vinegar.

Place the ricotta on a serving plate and spoon over the olive mixture. Serve warm.

SERVES 4 174 calories, 0.9g carbs, 17.2g fat, 4.5g sat fat, 3.8g protein

PEACH AND BASIL

1 fresh, ripe yellow or white peach, washed
4 tablespoons extra virgin olive oil
6–8 basil leaves, torn if large
1 x 150g burrata
sea salt and freshly cracked black pepper

Slice open the peach and remove the stone. Either tear or cut the peach into large pieces.

Place the peach in a bowl, drizzle over the oil and season with sea salt and freshly cracked black pepper. Stir in the basil.

Tear the burrata into large pieces, arrange on a serving plate and spoon over the peach mixture. Leave to stand for 10 minutes, then serve.

SERVES 4 191 calories, 2.2g carbs, 18g fat, 6.1g sat fat, 5.3g protein

POMEGRANATE AND PISTACHIO

75g pomegranate seeds
75g pistachio nuts, roughly chopped
4 tablespoons extra virgin olive oil
2 tablespoons pomegranate molasses
1 x 150g buffalo burrata
sea salt and freshly cracked black pepper

Place the pomegranate seeds in a bowl with the pistachio nuts, oil and molasses and stir. Season to taste.

Tear the burrata into large pieces, arrange on a serving plate and spoon over the pomegranate mixture. Leave to stand for 10 minutes, then serve.

SERVES 4 325 calories, 9.1g carbs, 28.4g fat, 7.5g sat fat, 8.6g protein

FIGS, THYME AND HONEY

3 tablespoons extra virgin olive oil
3 fresh, ripe figs, torn open
2 tablespoons thyme leaves
2 tablespoons clear honey
150g feta
freshly cracked black pepper

Heat the oil in a small frying pan. Sauté the figs for 3 minutes until they just start to plump up. Add the thyme leaves and honey and cook for a further minute. Season with black pepper.

Break the feta into 2–3 pieces, arrange on a serving plate and spoon over the fig mixture. Leave to stand for 5 minutes, then serve warm.

SERVES 4 285 calories, 28.6g carbs, 16.5g fat, 6.3g sat fat, 7.3g protein

TAHINI AND SESAME SEEDS

The Greeks and Mediterranean countries in the East have, like many Middle Eastern countries, embraced the sesame seed and, in particular, the sesame paste, tahini. Tahini is made from hulled sesame seeds and jars of it are recognised by their two separated mixtures – the oil and sesame paste. Before using, always ensure you mix the two together to either make the basic tahini sauce – to use in the chickpea purée hummus (see page 26) – or spread on bread and drizzle with honey. Look out for tahini mixed with honey as it's perfect for spreading on toast and topping with fruits – excellent for breakfast.

When using tahini paste, the brands vary; I have found the more traditional brands like Cypressa and Krinos, are thicker and need the liquid specified in my following recipes. When using more modern brands from organic shops, they are much runnier, so add the water or other liquids gradually when using.

The sesame seed is one of my favourite ingredients to add to recipes for texture and most of all to flavour food, starting from breakfast and snacks to main meal recipes. Sprinkle over breakfast eggs, yogurt, salad dressings, roasted vegetables and chicken dishes – I have used them in plenty of ways throughout this book, each time giving the final recipe an uplifting finish.

For the best flavour, toast the sesame seeds before using, even if you are going to roast the sesame seeds further in the recipe. Place the sesame seeds on a flat baking tray and roast in a preheated oven at 180°C/350°Fgas mark 4 for 10–15 minutes, check halfway through as it does not take long for them to burn completely. Cool and keep in a sealed jar, close at hand with all your other seasonings, such as salt and pepper.

BASIC TAHINI SAUCE

Serve this basic sauce with grilled meat or fish or simply in a bowl as part of a mezze spread.

3 tablespoons tahini paste
75ml water
juice of ½ lemon
1–2 tablespoons extra virgin olive oil
sea salt flakes
pitta bread or sesame flatbread, to serve

In a small bowl, whisk the tahini with the water until smooth. Add enough lemon juice to taste, then season with salt and whisk in half the oil.

Pour into a serving bowl, drizzle with the remaining oil and serve with toasted pitta bread or sesame flatbread.

PER 100G 324 calories, 0.5g carbs, 32.3g fat, 4.6g sat fat, 8.1g protein

DATES STUFFED WITH FETA AND SESAME SEEDS

These stuffed dates make an excellent aperitif finger food or alternative dinner party dessert.

12 medjool dates, pitted
115g feta, sliced
2 tablespoons tahini paste
50ml water
pinch of sea salt
2 tablespoons extra virgin olive oil
1–2 tablespoons toasted sesame seeds

Open out each date, and insert a slice of feta in the middle, then arrange on a serving plate. In a small bowl, whisk the tahini paste with the water until smooth, then sprinkle with the salt. Drizzle the tahini over the dates, top with a drizzle of oil, then finish with the sesame seeds and serve.

SERVES 6 224 calories, 20.8g carbs, 13.7g fat, 4.1g sat fat, 5.9g protein

Dates Stuffed with Feta and Sesame Seeds

Chilli-marinated Green Olives

BASIC OLIVE KNOW-HOW

As a child, when in Cyprus in late summer, I would watch and then help my paternal grandmother prepare early-season olives for brining. The small, tough green olives would be cracked between two stones and then placed in water for a week. Each day, the water was changed to remove the bitterness and finally they were drained, washed and then flavoured with slices of lemon, cracked coriander seeds and a bay leaf or two. They were then kept in a big jar of brine and used whenever needed. Ever since then I've had a taste for olives. As a cook, I use them with so many things, often chopped with anchovies and fennel and parsley and scattered over fish, pasta, chicken and lamb dishes.

Manzanilla – medium-sized with a good flesh-to-pit ratio, these plump green olives represent what most people think of as Spanish olives. In fact, so much so that another name for them is 'Spanish olive'. They're tangy and nutty, with a smooth texture.

Nafplion – these small green, Greek olives are often brine-cured and traditionally slit to allow the marinade to flavour the flesh.

Kalamata – this is the classic Greek olive from the Kalamata area of mainland Greece. Large, dark, smooth and meaty, they make a great table olive for snacking.

Castelvetrano – this plump, pale green olive from Sicily is very much in vogue right now, and with its fleshy texture and briny flavour it's one of my favourites to use in recipes. I prefer to pit my own olives, but as this variety is particularly time-consuming to smash and pit, if you find them already pitted, I would buy and keep in the cupboard or fridge.

Cailletier – these are those small black olives from Nice and the Riviera di Ponente that have been made famous by use in French Niçoise salads. They are small with a large pit and have a lovely sharp, rich flavour.

Which style of olive to use in cooking

Salt-cured black olives – these olives are recognised by their wrinkled skins, and are black olives. They are sold in jars, or vacuum-packed containers with no liquid. These olives are perfect served with cheese and bread as a simple meal. They are also good added to stews and braises.

Cracked olives – these olives are often green, and sold with a simple marinade, maybe just sliced lemons. These olives are often slightly bitter, but they are excellent chopped and mixed with herbs.

SAUTÉED OLIVES

Heat 1–2 tablespoons extra virgin olive oil in a frying pan, add 115g black or green olives of your choice and cook until they plump up. Add 1 teaspoon lightly crushed coriander seeds or 1 large rosemary sprig. Serve warm with small slices of bread or crackers as a lovely pre-dinner snack.

SERVES 4 48 calories, 0g carbs, 5.3g fat, 0.8g sat fat, 0.3g protein

CHILLI-MARINATED GREEN OLIVES

Drain a 225g jar of pitted olives in brine and place in a bowl with sliced lemons, or try adding a small sliced preserved lemon. Add 1 teaspoon chilli flakes or 1 teaspoon paprika. Mix with 2 tablespoons extra virgin olive oil and serve.

SERVES 4 76 calories, 0.4g carbs, 8.2g fat, 1.2g sat fat, 0.4g protein

DRIED BLACK OLIVES

Take 225g black olives and remove the pits – gently press with the side of your knife to split the flesh, then pull out the pit. Place on a baking tray and dry out in a low oven (150°C/300°F/gas mark 2) for 2 hours, until the olives are quite crisp. Once cooled, roughly chop or crush using a pestle and mortar. Keep in an airtight jar and use to sprinkle over grilled fish, meat or salads.

SERVES 4 58 calories, 0g carbs, 6.2g fat, 0.9g sat fat, 0.5g protein

GRAINS THAT ARE GOOD

The Mediterranean diet embraces grains – with pasta and breads made from buckwheat, rye, spelt and chestnut flours, and risottos and pilafs that use wholegrain rice, wheat berries, bulgur, and so on. Pasta, pizza and risotto provide us with some of the best comfort food in the world and, when you use ancient grains that haven't been processed and stripped of all their nutrients, you can enjoy it completely guilt-free. I love pasta, but it has to be the right kind. I like it when it's delicate and melts in the mouth and actually has flavour. I also enjoy making pasta, but I don't have all the correct equipment or four hands for when I want to roll out perfect lasagne sheets! Therefore, all the pasta recipes in this chapter are aimed at the minimum fuss home pasta cook who wants to have a go and achieve good results in the simplest way possible. It's incredible what you can create with a little flour and a little water, and sometimes a little egg, so do give it a try.

GRAINS

Bulgur – also known as burghul or bulgar, is a wheat produced from wheat berries, after they have been par-boiled, dried and then coarsely ground into pointy-shaped groats. This grain is rich in protein and minerals and, as it has already been par-boiled, cooks quickly. It is used to make the traditional eastern Mediterranean tabbouleh.

Rice – this has long been a staple in all Mediterranean diets. Italian food is unthinkable without risotto (which commonly uses short-grained arborio and medium-grained carnaroli rice), and similarly paella is the defining dish of Spain (short-grained calasparra and bomba types). The Greeks opt for a long-grained rice (white and brown) for their pilafs.

Farro – this is an ancient grain of common wheat. It is also a wholegrain and is often sold pearled or semi-pearled, which means that it has been partly cooked, and therefore cooks quite quickly. It has a nutty texture and is a little chewy when cooked and not soft and mushy.

Wheat berries – this is the whole grain of wheat, the whole kernel, before it is broken down and processed to make bulgur wheat or flour. The berries are very high in fibre and they're also a great source of potassium and iron. They need to be soaked before cooking, for at least 4 hours, and then cooked for about an hour until soft. Their cooked texture is chewy.

Freekeh – this is a young green wholewheat grain, and also an ancient grain that is very high in fibre and a good source of protein and essential nutrients. It is sold either whole or cracked and the latter means that it will cook more quickly.

Spelt – this is also an ancient wheat grain and was a staple food back in Roman times. It's rich in fibre and full of nutrients – during milling, a lot of its bran and germ are left intact. Spelt takes longer to cook than farro, but you can find it cracked, which means it will cook faster and to a creamier consistency.

GRAIN BOWLS

Although not strictly Mediterranean and more of a west coast American trend, grain bowls make the most of ancient grains in such a fresh, healthy, protein-rich way that I had to include some here. I've been serving these types of dishes to friends for quite a few years now. I find that it's also a great way to use up leftovers. Grain bowls are composed of a cooked grain, with roasted veg or salads from the A Salad and More chapter (page 120) and then topped with an egg or approximately 150g cooked fish or chicken or leftover lamb. The pilaf recipes that follow can also be used as the base for your grain bowl.

MIXED RICE PILAF WITH ROASTED SQUASH

Place 225g Rice Pilaf (page 58) in a bowl, warm or at room temperature, and top with 20g baby rocket or spinach leaves, seasoned with a drizzle of extra virgin olive oil. Finish with 3–4 pieces of Roasted Squash (page 148) and serve.

SERVES 1 413 calories, 56.3g carbs, 17.6g fat, 2.5g sat fat, 10.5g protein

FARRO AND FENNEL PILAF WITH ROASTED SWISS CHARD AND POACHED EGG

Place 150g Farro and Fennel Pilaf (page 59) in a bowl, warm or at room temperature, and mix in a portion of Sesame-roasted Swiss Chard (page 152). Transfer to a serving bowl and top either with a poached egg, or soft-boiled egg. Drizzle with extra virgin olive oil, scatter with toasted sesame seeds and serve.

SERVES 1 403 calories, 22.1g carbs, 29.1g fat, 5g sat fat, 14.1g protein

BULGUR PILAF WITH FENNEL SALAD AND CHICKEN

Flatten out 1–2 boneless, skinless chicken thighs and rub all over with a little extra virgin olive oil and a few pinches of sea salt and chilli flakes. Place under a hot grill and cook for 8 minutes on each side until tender. Place 150g Bulgur Pilaf (page 58) in a bowl, warm or at room temperature, and mix in a quarter portion of the Fennel and Hazelnut Salad (page 122). Top with the chicken thighs and serve with a fresh shaving of pecorino.

SERVES 1 569 calories, 37g carbs, 33.7g fat, 6.6g sat fat, 32.5g protein

Mixed Rice Pilaf with Roasted Squash

Recipe on left: Wheat Berries with Pomegranate
(see page 59); above: Moroccan preserved lemons;
below: Treviso; bottom right: Farro and Fennel Pilaf
(see page 59); Top right: grains – from the top: spelt;
farro; wheat berries; mixed brown rice; freekeh

BULGUR WHEAT PILAF

I grew up eating this pilaf with stews, grilled meats, fish or slow-cooked roasted meat. My family have always toasted the vermicelli before cooking starts, and I have since come across this method of toasting pasta within Spanish cooking too.

4 tablespoons extra virgin olive oil
1 onion, finely chopped
50g vermicelli
225g bulgur wheat
500ml chicken stock, dried mushroom water or water
25g flat-leaf parsley, chopped
sea salt and freshly cracked black pepper
Greek yogurt, to serve

Heat half the oil in a large sauté or risotto pan with a tight-fitting lid and cook the onion for 10 minutes until soft and starting to brown in places. Remove the onion and set aside.

Add the remaining oil to the pan. Crush the vermicelli once in your hand, then add to the hot oil and cook, stirring, until golden and toasted. Stir in the bulgur wheat and coat all the grains with the oil. Return the onion to the pan with the stock, bring to the boil, then reduce to a simmer. Cover the pan and cook for 15 minutes until the grains have swelled and all the liquid has been absorbed. Set aside with the lid on for 10 minutes.

Remove the lid and season with salt and pepper. Fluff up the grains with a fork and gently mix in the chopped parsley. Serve warm or cold with the thick Greek yogurt.

SERVES 6 359 calories, 58.1g carbs, 12.6g fat, 1.7g sat fat, 7.8g protein

MIXED RICE PILAF

Look for bags of mixed brown rice as these will also include some wild rice. I love to use Puy lentils here, but use whichever kind you like, except the small red or yellow ones that are used for Indian dhal. This is delicious served with roasted or grilled meat and fish.

10g dried mushrooms, such as trumpet, porcini and
  chanterelles
4 tablespoons extra virgin olive oil
1 onion, finely chopped
350g mixed brown rice, washed and strained through
  a sieve
150g Puy lentils, washed and strained through a sieve
50ml red wine
2 tablespoons chopped fresh dill or parsley
sea salt and freshly cracked black pepper

Place the mushrooms in a large measuring jug and cover with 750ml boiling water. Leave to stand for at least 10 minutes or up to an hour.

Lay a sheet of kitchen paper in the bottom of a sieve and place over a large bowl. Strain the mushrooms and reserve the liquid. Wash the mushrooms to remove any grit and pat dry, then finely chop and set aside.

Heat half the oil in a sauté or risotto pan and cook the onion for 5 minutes until soft but not browned. Add the rice and lentils and cook, stirring, for 3–5 minutes, until the grains are well coated with oil, then add the wine and simmer until all the liquid has evaporated.

Stir in 500ml of the reserved mushroom water, add the chopped mushrooms, then bring to the boil again and reduce to a simmer. Cook, partially covered, until the grains are tender, but still have a slight bite, about 40 minutes, adding extra liquid as and when required.

Season, drizzle with the remaining oil and scatter over herbs of your choice. Serve warm or at room temperature.

SERVES 6 355 calories, 60.1g carbs, 8.8g fat, 1.3g sat fat, 11.1g protein

FARRO AND FENNEL PILAF

For a very simple vegetable stock, I like to soak about 5–10g mixed dried mushrooms in boiling water for 10 minutes and then strain the liquid through a lined sieve. I then keep the mushrooms in a small container in the fridge and re-use them a few more times, or sometimes I include them in the recipe for extra flavour. This is another pilaf that goes beautifully with grilled meats, fish or poultry.

4 tablespoons extra virgin olive oil
1 onion, finely chopped
1 head of fennel or 2 heads of wild fennel, trimmed and
  finely chopped, reserving any fronds
350g farro, washed and strained through a sieve
500ml dried mushroom water or chicken stock
25g flat-leaf parsley, finely chopped
25g dill or fennel fronds, finely chopped
sea salt and freshly cracked black pepper

Heat half the oil in a large sauté or risotto pan and cook the onion and fennel for 10 minutes until soft and just beginning to caramelise. Stir in the farro and coat all the grains with the oil.

Add the mushroom water or chicken stock and bring to the boil, then reduce to a simmer and cook, partially covered, for 20 minutes until the farro is plump and tender but not mushy. If there is a little liquid left, it will be absorbed.

Season well with salt and pepper, stir through the herbs and drizzle with the remaining oil. Serve warm or at room temperature.

SERVES 6 175 calories, 21.9g carbs, 8.4g fat, 1.2g sat fat, 3.9g protein

WHEAT BERRIES WITH POMEGRANATE

You will find that some wheat berry varieties are much smaller than others. All need to be soaked prior to cooking, for at least an hour and ideally overnight. Their texture will be tender but also a little nutty to the bite.

3 tablespoons extra virgin olive oil, plus extra for drizzling
1 medium onion, chopped
350g wheat berries, soaked overnight and drained
1 litre water or light chicken stock
25g flat-leaf parsley, chopped
15g dill, chopped
50g blanched almonds, toasted
1 pomegranate, deseeded
3 tablespoons pomegranate molasses
150g feta, sliced
sea salt and freshly cracked black pepper

Heat the oil in a large sauté or risotto pan and cook the onion for 5 minutes until soft, then add the wheat berries and stir to coat with the oil.

Pour in the warm water or light chicken stock. Bring to the boil, reduce to a simmer and cook for 1½ hours until the grains are tender but still have a little bite, and the liquid has been absorbed.

With a slotted spoon for straining excess liquid, transfer the wheat berries to a large serving bowl or platter. While still warm, season with salt and pepper and stir through the herbs, almonds and pomegranate seeds and molasses. Top with the feta, drizzle with a little more oil and serve.

SERVES 4 595 calories, 67g carbs, 25.1g fat, 7.4g sat fat, 23.1g protein

CLASSIC PAELLA WITH FREEKEH

Here the chorizo gives the paella all the smoked paprika flavouring it requires. If making without chorizo, add 2 teaspoons smoked paprika to the dish when sautéing the onion.

a large pinch of saffron strands
2 tablespoons extra virgin olive oil
100g dried chorizo, skin removed and thinly sliced
3 boned chicken thighs, each cut into 3 pieces
1 large sweet onion, roughly chopped
2 celery sticks, chopped
2 garlic cloves, grated on a microplane
350g freekeh
750ml hot chicken or vegetable stock
small bunch of thyme, tied together
350g mussels
250g cockles or clams
225g raw prawns
25g flat-leaf parsley, finely chopped
sea salt and freshly cracked black pepper
lemon wedges, to serve

Place the saffron strands in a small cup, add 5 tablespoons of warm water and set aside to soak. Heat the oil in a large cast-iron pan and add the chorizo. Cook over a medium heat for 5 minutes until just browned. Remove and set aside.

Add the chicken thighs to the pan juices and brown for 3 minutes on each side, then remove and set aside.

Drain off all but 3 tablespoons of the pan juices and cook the onion and celery for 5 minutes until soft. Stir in the garlic and freekeh and cook for 1 minute, then add all the stock and bring to the boil. Add the saffron water, thyme, chicken and chorizo and season. Stir well, reduce the heat to a simmer, and cook, covered, for 20 minutes until the freekeh is almost tender and there is still a little liquid in the pan. Add all the shellfish, cover and cook for another 8 minutes, for the mussels and cockles to open and the prawns to turn pink. Serve immediately with a sprinkling of parsley and lemon wedges on the side.

SERVES 6 460 calories, 40.9g carbs, 14.8g fat, 3.5g sat fat, 42.9g protein

SQUID INK FREEKEH

This recipe is based on the Spanish method of cooking paella, but uses freekeh instead of rice. The type of pancetta or smoked cured meat that you use will have a big influence on the flavour of the dish; sometimes I use guanciale.

1 pouch or 2 tablespoons squid or cuttlefish ink
50g pancetta
1 onion, finely chopped
225g freekeh, washed and drained
2 tablespoons extra virgin olive oil
6 spring onions
500g squid, cleaned, with legs and bodies separated and large bodies cut into rings
1 large Brandywine/or Kumato heritage tomato, chopped
2 tablespoons red wine vinegar
sea salt and freshly cracked black pepper

In a bowl, mix the ink with 500ml water, then transfer to a saucepan and bring gently to the boil.

In a sauté pan, render the pancetta in its own fat until almost crisp, then lay on a few sheets of kitchen paper and set aside. Drain off all but 2 tablespoons of the pancetta fat from the pan, then sauté the onion for 5 minutes until soft, and stir in the freekeh, coating the grains with the oil. Add the ink stock, stir, cover and simmer for 20 minutes until the freekeh is almost tender. Remove the lid, stir, season and cook, uncovered, for a further 5 minutes until all the liquid is absorbed.

Meanwhile, heat a cast-iron grill pan until smoking. Grease with a little of the oil, then char the spring onions for 2 minutes on each side to blacken. Set aside. Season the squid with salt, pepper and a drizzle of olive oil, then cook on the grill pan for about 2 minutes on each side until charred. The legs should curl up and go pink.

Transfer the squid to a bowl, add the tomato, vinegar and any remaining oil and toss to mix. Divide the freekeh between serving bowls and top with the squid and spring onions.

SERVES 6 263 calories, 26g carbs, 8.1g fat, 1.6g sat fat, 22.6g protein

Squid Ink Freekeh

Borlotti Bean and Radicchio Spelt Risotto

RISOTTO

The beauty of a risotto is you can take the basic recipe and easily adapt it to reflect the season you're in and the delicious produce that is available. The key to a good risotto is in the perfect, mellow balancing of all the layers of flavour that come from the vegetables, stock, grains and cheese. You definitely need to use a good-quality stock, be it chicken, fish, shellfish or vegetable, and the right pan can also make all the difference. I was taught to use a sauté pan, which is wider than a regular saucepan and slightly deeper than a frying pan, and provides a good surface area so that the grains can cook evenly in the stock and the liquid can move around the pan and evaporate evenly.

Using the spelt risotto recipe (to the right) as your base, vary the grains and ingredients as per the season and try out these combinations.

PEA AND FENNEL

Replace the red wine with white wine. Use farro in place of the cracked spelt. Add 1 small head of fennel, trimmed and finely chopped, with the onion. Add 150g fresh or frozen peas (if frozen, soaked in warm water until defrosted) and 100g sugar snap peas, trimmed and sliced, to the risotto 10 minutes before the end of cooking. Continue as per the recipe and sprinkle with basil to serve.

SERVES 4 528 calories, 41.3g carbs, 31.2g fat, 13.8g sat fat, 19.2g protein

SAUSAGE AND BROCCOLI RAPINI

Remove the casing from 175g Italian fennel or spicy sausages and crumble the filling into the pan with the onion. Cook until the sausage meat has a touch of colour. Continue as per the recipe, using freekeh or whole spelt as the grain. Towards the final 10 minutes of cooking, stir in 225g broccoli rapini (or other greens or sprouting broccoli), washed and chopped into 2.5cm pieces. Continue as per the recipe.

SERVES 6 519 calories, 41.5g carbs, 28.7g fat, 11.6g sat fat, 24.1g protein

BORLOTTI BEAN AND RADICCHIO SPELT RISOTTO

This creamy-textured autumn-flavoured risotto is made with cracked spelt. Most people cook these ancient grains first in boiling water, before adding them to a dish, however, I like to incorporate the liquid that they are cooked in as it gives more of a rounded flavour. If using regular, non-cracked spelt, cook for longer, adding more liquid as well.

1.2 litres stock or dried mushroom water
4 tablespoons extra virgin olive oil
2 garlic cloves, bashed to split the skins
1 large onion, chopped
350g cracked spelt
50ml good-quality red wine
200g fresh podded borlotti beans
50g unsalted butter
100g pecorino, finely grated, plus extra to serve
100g radicchio, sliced
sea salt and freshly cracked black pepper

Place the stock or mushroom water in a deep stockpot and bring to the boil, then reduce the heat and keep on a gentle simmer.

Heat half the oil in a sauté or risotto pan and cook the garlic cloves until golden, then remove and discard. Add the onion to the pan and cook for 5 minutes until soft, then stir in the spelt, coating each grain with the oil. Add the wine and simmer, stirring, until all of it has evaporated. Add half the stock and the borlotti beans, stir and cook, partially covered, for 10 minutes until the liquid is absorbed. Keep stirring and adding stock for about 25 minutes, until the beans are cooked and the spelt is creamy and tender.

Remove the pan from the heat, add the butter and stir to melt. Stir in the cheese and radicchio, cover the pan and leave to stand for 5 minutes. Season well to taste and serve drizzled with the remaining oil.

SERVES 4 508 calories, 37g carbs, 31g fat, 13.6g sat fat, 18.2g protein

RISI BISI WITH FARRO

This Venetian risotto is one of my favourites – a classic spring risotto that makes the most of an abundance of fresh young herbs and vegetables. Although it is classically made with Venetian risotto rice, called *vialone nano*, here I've chosen to use farro, so technically it should be called farro bisi!

750ml chicken or vegetable stock
2 tablespoons extra virgin olive oil, plus extra for drizzling
2 garlic cloves, bashed to split the skins
2 shallots, finely chopped
6 spring onions, white and green parts separated, whites chopped
225g farro, washed and drained
225g large spinach leaves, washed
4 tarragon sprigs
15g flat-leaf parsley, chopped
500g fresh peas, podded or 300g frozen peas, defrosted
175g asparagus, cut into 2.5cm pieces
15g unsalted butter
50g finely grated Parmesan, plus extra to serve
sea salt and freshly cracked black pepper

Place the stock in a deep stockpot and bring to the boil, then reduce the heat and keep on a gentle simmer.

Heat the oil in a large sauté or risotto pan, add the garlic and cook until it starts to sizzle and flavour the oil, then remove and discard. Add the shallots and chopped spring onions (white parts) to the pan and cook gently until they soften, then stir in the farro so each grain is coated with the oil.

Add the hot stock, about four ladles at a time, stirring after each addition and then partially covering the pan until the liquid has been absorbed. The process is not exactly the same as when using risotto rice, but you do not want the grains to become mushy, so this is a good way of keeping tabs on it. Cook for about 25 minutes over a medium heat until the farro is tender but retains a little bite.

Meanwhile, place the green spring onion stalks, spinach and herbs in a food-processor or blender, add 2 ladles of stock and whizz until very smooth.

For the final 10 minutes of simmering, stir the green purée through the farro and season to taste. When the grains are just tender, with not too much bite, add the peas and asparagus and cook for 4 minutes. Add the butter and Parmesan and a ladleful of stock to loosen the mix if necessary, then remove from the heat and cover. Leave to rest for 3 minutes.

Uncover, stir the risotto and check for seasoning. Serve with extra Parmesan and cracked black pepper and a final drizzle of extra virgin olive oil.

SERVES 4 313 calories, 29.9g carbs, 15.5g fat, 5.6g sat fat, 15.4g protein

Risi Bisi with Farro

HAND-SHAPED PASTA

My mission is to make pasta special again as, of course, there is a world of difference between a bowl of homemade, hand-shaped pasta that makes you want to savour every bite, and a packet of dried pasta that you've cooked in 10 minutes with a bad supermarket sauce. There is so much possibility with pasta, as you can experiment with endless varieties of flours and flavourings, and even though using spelt or semolina or chestnut flour doesn't necessarily make it gluten-free, you are most likely using a higher-grade form of gluten, which leads to far fewer digestive problems.

SEMOLINA PASTA

For a pasta that has a robust texture and a little more bite, I recommend a rustic village-style pasta; pici from Tuscany or orecchiette or cavatelli from Puglia.

225g durum semolina flour
225g 00 flour
½ teaspoon fine sea salt
2 teaspoons extra virgin olive oil
250ml warm water

Mix the flours and salt together in a bowl, then heap the mixture onto a clean, dry worktop. Make a well in the centre and gradually add the oil and water, mixing the dry ingredients into the centre before adding more liquid and starting to knead as the dough forms. The dough will feel quite rough and tough even when all the liquid has been added. Start to knead for about 10 minutes or until it becomes smooth and springs back when gently pressed with your index finger.

Cover the dough completely with clingfilm and leave to rest for 30 minutes at room temperature. It can rest overnight in the fridge too. Bring back to room temperature before shaping.

PER 100G 231 calories, 49.9g carbs, 1.7g fat, 0.3g sat fat, 7g protein

To shape cavatelli Divide the dough into six equal pieces, then cover with a clean tea-towel. Line a baking tray with another clean tea-towel and sprinkle with a little more flour or durum semolina flour. Take one piece of dough and use your hands to roll into a long, thin sausage strand, about 1cm thick, then cut into 3cm long pieces. Using the tips of your index finger and middle finger, flatten each piece of dough with your fingers and then roll/drag the piece of dough towards you. It will become slightly longer than it started with a curled centre. Place on the prepared lined baking tray. Continue with the rest of the dough and, when all the pasta is shaped, keep in a cool, dry place for 30 minutes or in the fridge. Alternatively, you can freeze the pasta on the tray and then transfer to ziplock bags. You can also cook straight from frozen, adding only a few extra minutes to the cooking time.

To shape orecchiette Divide the dough into eight pieces and, working with one piece at a time, use your hands to roll each into a log about 1.5cm thick. Cut each log into discs, about 5mm thick. Place each disc flat on the worktop and, using a round-tipped knife dipped in flour, press down on the pasta, and drag towards you, to form a disc with a dent in the middle, shaped a little like an ear (orecchiette, of course, means little ears!). Alternatively, you can use your thumb, floured, to press into the centre of each disc, and twist your hand to make an indent. Allow to stand in a cool, dry place for 30 minutes before cooking, or freeze until required.

To shape pici Pici dough is the same used for both cavatelli and orecchiette, but it is rolled into long thin strands. Take a walnut-sized piece of dough and roll out with your fingers into long strands about 5mm thick. Cut into lengths about 20cm long. Do not hang to dry but allow to lay flat.

To cook To cook any of the above pasta, bring a large pot of salted water to the boil and add a drop of oil to the pot. Cook the pasta in two batches. Start timing from when the pasta floats to the top; cook for about 15 minutes. Remember to reserve about 150ml pasta water to add to the sauce. Serve with any one of the sauces on pages 70–73.

EGG PASTA

Making pasta with eggs results in a light-textured pasta, with an almost melt-in-the-mouth finish. Experiment with using different flours such as buckwheat, rye, chestnut and chickpea as each lends its own distinctive flavour – chickpea and buckwheat are quite earthy, chestnut is sweet and nutty, etc. These flours are delicate and can easily be rolled out with a rolling pin and then cut into triangles or squares or into discs with a small cookie cutter.

100g chickpea, chestnut, buckwheat or rye flour
200g 00 flour
½ teaspoon fine salt
1 teaspoon extra virgin olive oil
2–3 medium eggs
semolina flour, for dusting

Mix the flours and salt together in a bowl and rub in the olive oil, then heap the mixture onto a clean, dry worktop. Make a well in the centre, crack in the first egg and use the tips of your fingers to incorporate it with the flour. When dry, add the second egg, mixing in again with your fingertips. Repeat with the third egg (adding a little at a time this time), continuing to mix until the mixture binds together. Knead for 10 minutes until the dough becomes springy and smooth. Wrap in clingfilm and set aside for 1 hour in the fridge.

Divide the dough into four and, using a rolling pin on a well-floured surface, roll out each piece to the thickness of 2mm. Cut the pasta into 5cm-thick ribbons for pappardelle, or cut into triangles, squares or discs. Transfer to a tray lined with a clean tea-towel. Allow to stand for 30 minutes.

This pasta is delicate; to cook, place in a large pot of boiling salted water. The pasta will sink to the bottom. Once it rises to the top, cook for 2–3 minutes, then drain. Use with any of the sauces on pages 70-73.

PER 100G 274 calories, 50.9g carbs, 4.5g fat, 1.1g sat fat, 10.7g protein

SQUID-INK PASTA

I have bought dried squid-ink pasta. And if you've done the same, you probably agree that it's a waste of time and money. One of my favourite food memories is of a squid-ink pici-noodle that I tasted on one of my work trips in Italy. It was served very simply with black pepper, lemon and salty pecorino and it tasted intensely of the ocean. It is worth making your own and it's essential to find proper squid or cuttlefish ink. It's sold in jars or pouches, and you often find it in delis, rather than fishmongers. There are cheap brands, but you get what you pay for and the pricier ones have the better flavour.

550g 00 flour
1 teaspoon fine sea salt
2 teaspoons extra virgin olive oil
2 tablespoons squid or cuttlefish ink
1 medium egg, plus 1 egg yolk

Place the flour in the bowl of a stand mixer and mix in the salt. Add the oil and mix to form a light crumb-like texture. Beat the squid or cuttlefish ink and egg and egg yolk together in a bowl, then add to the flour and mix to form a shaggy dough.

Change to a dough hook and knead the dough for 10 minutes until it becomes smooth and springs back when gently pressed with your index finger. Cover with clingfilm and chill in the fridge for 30 minutes.

If making by hand, mix the flour and salt together, heap the mixture onto a clean, dry worktop and make a well in the centre. Beat together the oil, ink and eggs and egg yolk, gradually, pour into the well and use the tips of your fingers to bring dry flour into the wet mixture until you have a shaggy dough. Knead for 10 minutes until smooth and it springs back when gently pressed with your index finger. Cover with clingfilm and chill for 30 minutes.

Divide the dough into six pieces and, while using one piece, keep the others covered. Use to make long pasta noodles of your choice – pici or pappardelle.

PER 100G 324g calories, 66.3g carbs, 3.5g fat, 0.8g sat fat, 11.2g protein

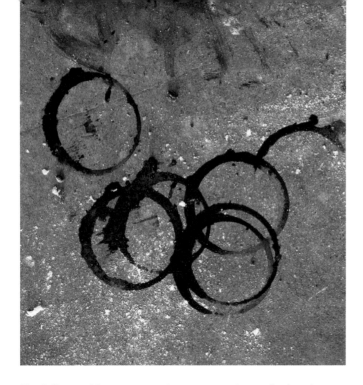

Far left: cooking egg pasta rags; centre: rolled-out egg pasta rags; top right: top of the tray – cavatelli, bottom of the tray – orecchiette; bottom right: squid-ink pici

GUANCIALE, EGG AND BROCCOLI RAPINI

100g guanciale, cubed
6 eggs, beaten
225g broccoli rapini, chopped into bite-sized pieces
350g hand-shaped pasta (triangles), cooked and drained
  (see pages 66–67)
25–50g finely grated pecorino or Parmesan
extra virgin olive oil, to serve

Cook the guanciale in a large frying pan to render all the fat; set aside. Remove all but 2 tablespoons of the fat and return to the heat. Slowly scramble the eggs in the pan juices, then add the broccoli and cook for 5 minutes.

Stir in the cooked pasta and a little pasta cooking water to keep the mixture loose. Season to taste. Divide between serving plates and top with cheese. Drizzle with a little extra virgin olive oil to serve.

SERVES 4 447 calories, 45.6g carbs, 19g fat, 6.9g sat fat, 27g protein

COCKLES AND ESCAROLE

4 tablespoons extra virgin olive oil
2 garlic cloves, grated on a microplane
500g cockles or small clams
225g escarole or dandelion leaves, cut into 10cm pieces
350g pici pasta, cooked and drained (see page 66)
juice of 1 lemon
50g finely grated Parmesan

Heat half the oil in a large frying pan, stir in the garlic and sizzle for 2 minutes. Stir in the cockles, cover and cook for 5 minutes until the shells start to open.

Stir through the escarole and cook for a further 3–4 minutes until wilted. Add the pasta and lemon juice, toss to mix, add a little reserved cooking water, season and bring to a simmer. Divide the pasta and sauce between serving bowls and serve with a sprinkling of Parmesan and a drizzle of the remaining oil.

SERVES 4 455 calories, 48.8g carbs, 17.6g fat, 4.4g sat fat, 28.1g protein

CHAR-GRILLED SQUID AND ROCKET

500g squid, cleaned, with heads and bodies separated
2 tablespoons extra virgin olive oil, plus extra to serve
6 spring onions, chopped
350g squid-ink pasta (pici) (see page 67), cooked and
    drained
150g rocket, chopped
lemon slices, to serve

Slice the squid bodies into 1cm-thick rings. Heat the oil in a
large frying pan and stir-fry all the squid for 3–4 minutes until
almost tender. Stir in the spring onions, season and cook for
3 minutes – the squid tentacles should turn bright pink.

Add the pici pasta and 100ml pasta cooking water. Stir well and
bring to a simmer, then remove from the heat and stir through
the rocket. Serve with lemon slices and a final drizzle of olive oil.

SERVES 4 445 calories, 60g carbs, 10.9g fat, 2.1g sat fat, 30.7g protein

RICOTTA WITH ASPARAGUS AND PEA SHOOTS

2 small shallots, finely sliced
juice of 1 lemon
2 tablespoons extra virgin olive oil, plus extra to serve
350g asparagus, trimmed and cut into 3cm pieces
350g chestnut flour pasta rags, cooked and drained
150g pea shoots
150g fresh ricotta, drained

Place the shallots and lemon juice in a bowl and leave to stand
for 5 minutes. Heat the oil in a large frying pan and sauté the
asparagus for 3 minutes. Add the shallot mixture to the pan
and continue to cook until the asparagus is tender, adding a
little pasta cooking water, if necessary.

Stir in the cooked pasta rags, toss in the pea shoots and
season. Divide between serving bowls and top with a heaped
tablespoon of ricotta. Serve with an extra drizzle of olive oil.

SERVES 4 376 calories, 47.6g carbs, 14.5g fat, 4.6g sat fat, 16.8g protein

BUTTERNUT SQUASH AND SAGE

300g peeled, deseeded butternut squash pieces
3 tablespoons extra virgin olive oil, plus extra for drizzling
2 shallots, chopped
½ teaspoon Calabrian chilli flakes
75g almonds or walnuts, toasted and chopped
3 tablespoons finely chopped sage
350g hand-shaped pasta (orecchiette or cavatelli), cooked and drained (see page 66)
75g finely grated Parmesan

Using a food-processor, shred the butternut squash. Heat the olive oil in a large frying pan, add the shallots and chilli flakes and cook for 3 minutes. Stir in the squash and sauté for 3 minutes. Stir in 150ml pasta water, cover and cook for 10 minutes. Add the nuts, sage and cooked pasta and simmer, stirring well. Remove from the heat and season. Stir in the Parmesan; drizzle with olive oil to serve.

SERVES 4 505 calories, 52.4g carbs, 26.3g fat, 6g sat fat, 18.2g protein

MUSSELS AND TOMATOES

4 tablespoons extra virgin olive oil, plus extra to serve
2 shallots, chopped
500g cherry tomatoes
½ teaspoon Calabrian chilli flakes (optional)
3–4 flat-leaf parsley sprigs, plus extra chopped to serve
750g mussels
100ml dry white wine
350g hand-shaped pasta (buckwheat pappardelle), cooked and drained (see page 67)

Heat the oil in a large sauté pan and add the shallots, tomatoes, chilli flakes (if using) and parsley sprigs. Stir in the mussels and white wine, then cover and cook for 10 minutes, stirring once. Once the mussels have opened and the tomatoes have popped, taste and season. Toss in the cooked pasta and a little extra pasta cooking water, if needed (the mixture should be brothy). Divide between serving bowls, sprinkle with chopped parsley and drizzle with olive oil to serve.

SERVES 4 489 calories, 53.5g carbs, 16.6g fat, 2.7g sat fat, 30.5g protein

SIMPLE LEMON SAUCE

50g butter
100g finely grated Parmesan cheese, plus extra to serve
finely grated zest and juice of 1–2 lemons
350g pasta (cavatelli or orecchiette), cooked and drained
  (see page 66)
extra virgin olive oil and 4 seared lemon halves, to serve

Melt the butter in a wok-style frying pan and add the cheese; whisk until the cheese melts. Gradually whisk in 150ml pasta cooking water to form an emulsion and continue whisking as you add the lemon zest and juice of 1 lemon. Season to taste, then add the pasta and toss to coat.

Check for seasoning and add more lemon juice if required. Serve immediately with extra Parmesan, a drizzle of olive oil and the seared lemon halves on the side.

SERVES 4 409 calories, 44.1g carbs, 20g fat, 12.1g sat fat, 16.2g protein

CRISPY ANCHOVY BREADCRUMBS

5 tablespoons extra virgin olive oil, plus extra to serve
2 salted anchovies, filleted (see page 34)
1 garlic clove, grated on a microplane
1 teaspoon Calabrian chilli flakes
150g stale bread, processed to make fine breadcrumbs
3 tablespoons thyme leaves
4 tablespoons finely grated Parmesan, plus extra to serve
350g hand-shaped pasta (orecchiette or cavatelli), cooked
  and drained (see page 66)

Heat the oil in a frying pan and add the anchovies, garlic and chilli flakes, stirring until the anchovies dissolve into the oil. Add the breadcrumbs and cook over a low heat for 10–15 minutes until crisp and golden. Stir in the thyme, Parmesan and cooked pasta. Let the pasta brown a little, adding a little more oil if needed. If too dry, add 3–4 tablespoons of pasta cooking water. Serve with Parmesan and a drizzle of olive oil.

SERVES 4 488 calories, 63.3g carbs, 21g fat, 5.4g sat fat, 16g protein

PIZZA DOUGH

Pizza is never out of fashion, even these days with everyone going low-carb and gluten-free! As with almost all Italian food, it can encompass huge variety and so, while in Rome, I've eaten some of the thinnest-crusted pizza ever, which was almost like a cracker, whereas down in southern Italy they serve a bouncier, sourdough-style crust that is also delicious. The lazy cook in me means I buy my pizza dough, then continue to prepare my bases. In New York, I buy my pizza dough, fresh or frozen from Wholefoods or Eately. In London, it's my local pizzeria in Newington Green.

PIZZA BASE

350g pizza dough of your choice, at room temperature
flour, for dusting
finely ground semolina, for dusting (optional)
2 tablespoons extra virgin olive oil

Preheat the oven to 240°C/475°F/gas mark 9 and place a pizza stone in the hottest part of the oven – for convection fan ovens this is in the middle, for non-convection it's the top.

Divide the dough into two and work with both pieces at the same time, allowing one to rest while working with the other. First dust your rolling pin with a little flour and roll the dough out into a rough circle. Then, working from the centre, use your fingers to stretch the dough out to a diameter of approximately 25cm. Place the pizza dough on a big sheet of parchment paper, or sprinkle a large, flat baking tray with semolina and place the dough on top. Allow the dough to rest for 5 minutes.

Prick the base all over with a fork, to allow the dough to rise evenly, then brush lightly with olive oil and slide the dough onto the pizza stone. Bake for 2–3 minutes until just set. If any large air bubbles pop up, just press them down with a fork.

Top the pizza base with your choice of topping (see right and pages 76–77).

MAKES 2 475 calories, 78.8g carbs, 13.6g fat, 2.1g sat fat, 14.3g protein

Pizza toppings

BUTTERNUT SQUASH, KALE AND WALNUT

This is a white or blanco pizza, meaning there is no tomato sauce to cover the base and the toppings are layered straight onto the pizza dough. The butternut squash is thinly sliced on a mandolin so that it cooks fast. You may need to bake your pizzas one after the other.

500g Tuscan kale, cut into 2.5cm pieces
1 red onion, thinly sliced on a mandolin
2 garlic cloves, grated on a microplane
juice of 1 lemon
4 tablespoons extra virgin olive oil
350g peeled, deseeded butternut squash, thinly sliced on a mandolin
2 pre-cooked pizza bases
150g buffalo ricotta
2 x 150g mozzarella balls
75g walnut pieces
sea salt and freshly cracked black pepper
Calabrian chilli flakes, grated Parmesan and dried oregano, to serve

Preheat the oven to 240°C/475°F/gas mark 9 and place a pizza stone on the middle shelf to preheat.

Place the kale, onion, garlic, lemon juice, 2 tablespoons olive oil and seasoning in a bowl and toss together to coat the leaves well. Leave to stand for 10 minutes. Add the butternut squash and toss once more to coat the squash with the flavourings.

Spread each pizza base with the ricotta and then pile the vegetable mixture on top.

Tear the mozzarella, and divide between the pizzas. Scatter the walnuts on top, drizzle with the remaining oil and bake for 20–25 minutes until the squash is tender and caramelised and the cheese is bubbling. Serve sprinkled with chilli flakes, Parmesan and dried oregano.

SERVES 4 801 calories, 53.3g carbs, 52.1g fat, 17.2g sat fat, 33.2g protein

Butternut Squash, Kale and Walnut

RICOTTA, MUSHROOM AND BITTER LEAVES

2 pre-cooked pizza bases
150g fresh ricotta, drained
100g chopped mixed escarole, dandelion or rocket leaves
225g mixed mushrooms, such as shiitake, portobello,
   conventional white capped, hen of the wood, trumpet
   etc., brushed clean and thinly sliced
2 tablespoons extra virgin olive oil, plus extra to serve
50g finely grated Parmesan
2 medium eggs
sea salt and freshly cracked black pepper
Calabrian chilli flakes, to serve

Preheat the oven to 240°C/475°F/gas mark 9 and place a pizza stone on the middle shelf to preheat.

Spread the pizza bases with ricotta. Place the greens and mushrooms in a large bowl and dress with the oil, half the Parmesan and season. Toss together well, then pile onto the ricotta and crack an egg on top of each pizza.

Bake for 15–20 minutes until the base is crisp and golden; the eggs should still be runny, but cook a touch longer if you prefer them well done. Drizzle with a little extra olive oil and scatter with chilli flakes and the remaining Parmesan to serve.

SERVES 4 434 calories, 40.4g carbs, 22.6g fat, 7.5g sat fat, 19.9g protein

TOMATO, ANCHOVIES AND MOZZARELLA

1kg red cherry tomatoes
2 large basil sprigs, plus extra leaves to serve
1 small shallot, finely chopped
splash of dry white wine
pinch of sugar
2 pre-cooked pizza bases
500g mixed multi-coloured small tomatoes, halved or
   sliced, depending on size
2 x 150g buffalo mozzarella balls, torn
8 anchovy fillets in oil
drizzle of extra virgin olive oil, for drizzling
sea salt flakes and freshly cracked black pepper

In a pan, place the cherry tomatoes with the basil, shallot, wine and sugar. Bring to a simmer, cover and cook for 30 minutes until the tomatoes have burst and cooked down. Season to taste with salt and pepper and discard the basil.

Preheat the oven to 240°C/475°F/gas mark 9 and place a pizza stone on the middle shelf to preheat.

Spread the pizza bases with the tomato sauce and top with the multi-coloured tomatoes, mozzarella and anchovies. Season, drizzle with a little olive oil and bake for 20 minutes until the cheese is melted and bubbling, the tomatoes have started to caramelise and the base is crisp and golden. Drizzle with a little extra olive oil and sprinkle with basil to serve.

SERVES 4 540 calories, 53g carbs, 25.5g fat, 12g sat fat, 27.9g protein

PRESERVED LEMON, RICOTTA AND THYME

This is not quite a pizza as we know it, but these are all the flavours I like about the Mediterranean and can be served as an appetiser instead of a main meal pizza – preserved lemons, fresh thyme, ricotta and lots of extra virgin olive oil. If lemon thyme is available, use that as an option, in place of common thyme.

2 pre-baked pizza bases
4 tablespoons extra virgin olive oil
150g fresh ricotta, drained
4 preserved lemons
15g thyme sprigs
2 garlic cloves, thinly sliced on a mandolin
25g pitted salt-cured black olives
2 tablespoons finely grated Parmesan
1 teaspoon Calabrian chilli flakes (optional)
sea salt and freshly cracked black pepper

Preheat the oven to 240°C/475°F/gas mark 9 and place a pizza stone on the middle shelf to preheat.

Brush the pizza bases with some of the extra virgin olive oil. Spread the bases with ricotta. Season with freshly cracked black pepper. Thinly slice the preserved lemons, discard any seeds, then divide between the bases.

Remove the thyme leaves from the sprigs and scatter all over the lemons, followed by the garlic and olives. Drizzle with half the remaining oil.

Bake for 15 minutes until the base is crisp and the topping is bubbling. Cut into quarters and sprinkle with Parmesan, chilli flakes (if using) and drizzle with the remaining extra virgin olive oil to serve.

SERVES 4 108 kcal, 10.5g carbs, 6g fat, 1.6g sat fat, 3.3g protein

TOMATO, COPPA AND ROCKET

This is a twist on the classic pepperoni pizza. Of course, you can use pepperoni, but I almost prefer thin slices of coppa, as they seem to melt into the tomato sauce and cheese.

1kg red cherry tomatoes
2 large basil sprigs
1 small shallot, finely chopped
splash of dry white wine
pinch of sugar
2 pre-cooked pizza bases
150g rocket or baby spinach leaves, roughly chopped
  if large
150g sliced coppa salami
2 x 150g buffalo mozzarella balls, torn
drizzle of extra virgin olive oil, plus extra to serve
sea salt and freshly cracked black pepper
Calabrian chilli flakes, to serve

In a pan, place the cherry tomatoes with the basil, shallot, wine and sugar. Bring to a simmer, cover and cook for 30 minutes until the tomatoes have burst and cooked down. Season to taste with salt and pepper and discard the basil.

Preheat the oven to 240°C/475°F/gas mark 9 and place a pizza stone on the middle shelf to preheat.

Spread the pizza bases with the tomato sauce, top with the rocket or spinach and season well. Finish with the coppa and mozzarella, drizzle with olive oil and bake for 20 minutes until the cheese is melted and bubbling and the base is crisp. Drizzle with a little extra olive oil and sprinkle with chilli flakes to serve.

SERVES 4 669 calories, 49.4g carbs, 38.9g fat, 17.2g sat fat, 33.2g protein

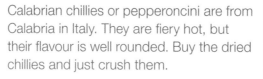

Calabrian chillies or pepperoncini are from Calabria in Italy. They are fiery hot, but their flavour is well rounded. Buy the dried chillies and just crush them.

Tomato, Coppa and Rocket (recipe on page 77)

TO BARBECUE/GRILL OR SEAR OR ROAST?
MEAT, FISH, SHELLFISH AND POULTRY

For me, cooking meat, poultry, fish and shellfish to perfection is all about mastering a few very simple methods. Be it grilling or, as we say in the UK, barbecuing, or pan-searing, which then leads to pan-roasting, or cooking 'en papillote' (meaning enclosed in a pouch or parcel)– these all allow you to cook your choice of protein in an incredibly quick, healthy and delicious way. I have included a variety of marinades and simple sauces that can be mixed and matched with the fish, chicken and meats, constantly thinking about variety – some traditional, some with a twist. Having a few simple staples in the store cupboard or fridge makes all the ideas very easily accessible – olives, anchovies, capers, lemons, flat-leaf parsley, garlic, shallots and red wine vinegar, chilli flakes (Calabrian, for me) and, of course, always extra virgin olive oil. Having a few dried herbs is important too – dried oregano, mint and rosemary are just as classic as they are fresh in different recipes.

LAMB CUTS

Rib chops – these are recognised by their long thin bone on one side. Sometimes, this type of chop is 'Frenched', when the meat is removed from the bone and then referred to as lollipop chops.

Loin chops – these have meat on both sides of a central bone. They can be a little fattier and so are suitable for slow cooking as well as fast searing or barbecuing.

Leg chops – these have the small round bone in the centre of the chop. Young or new season lamb leg chops are very meaty and so are excellent for barbecuing, or pan-searing and then finishing off in the oven.

Lamb sirloin steak – this is actually cut from the lower part of the leg (not the shank). The bone is removed and the meat opened out. You can flatten it out further by placing it between sheets of parchment paper and bashing it with a rolling pin.

Tenderloin – this is very lean and needs minimal cooking; ideally marinate in an oil-based marinade.

Shoulder of lamb – this cut is good for barbecuing as it is well marbled with fat, which means it will cook and remain very moist. I recommend you remove the bone, cut the meat into 3cm pieces and use for lamb souvlaki or shish!

Minced lamb – like shoulder of lamb, this has a good amount of fat, so season well and use to make koftes either in a pan, on the barbecue or under the grill.

BARBECUED LAMB RIB CHOPS WITH ROSEMARY AND CHERRY TOMATOES

As much as I love the look of a 'Frenched' lamb rib chop, I do find that the bone burns over the charcoal; therefore, opt for rib chops that still have the meat all down the bone. An alternative to barbecuing is searing the chops in a cast-iron pan for 3 minutes on each side. The tomatoes can also be pan-seared until they start to char and blister.

12 lamb rib chops, trimmed of some excess fat
1 quantity Za'atar-style Marinade (see page 85)
4 sprigs of small cherry tomatoes on the vine (about
　20 tomatoes in total) – whichever kind are in season
sea salt flakes and freshly cracked black pepper
flat-leaf parsley sprigs, to garnish
grain pilaf (see pages 58–59) and chopped salad, to serve

Prepare the charcoal barbecue and brush the grill rack with oil.

In a large, shallow dish, place the lamb chops and rub all over with half the marinade. Cover and allow to stand at room temperature for 30 minutes. Gently rub the cherry tomatoes, still on the vine, with half the remaining marinade.

Place the marinated lamb over the hot charcoal and grill for 3 minutes on each side.

Transfer to a large serving platter, cover with a tent of foil and allow to rest for 5 minutes.

Meanwhile, place a cooling rack over the grill rack on the barbecue, brush with oil once more, add the tomatoes, and season with salt and freshly cracked black pepper. The tomatoes will char almost immediately so remove them quickly and place over the lamb chops. Sprinkle with more sea salt flakes, scatter with fresh parsley and serve.

SERVES 4 546 calories, 2.3g carbs, 47.8g fat, 17.8g sat fat, 27.8g protein

Grilled Lamb Chops with Rosemary and Cherry Tomatoes

BACK TO BASICS

Mediterranean grilling or barbecuing is about simple, easy cooking. It's all about going back to basics and it's certainly not about big joints of meat or elaborate pulled pork. Most people cook over a charcoal fire and so the flavour of the charcoal is very important (and so delicious that often it's all you need). I grew up eating souvlaki – skewered meat, without any fancy veg on the skewers. This was then tucked into pitta bread with chopped salad and a dollop of tahini sauce, and that was it. But it was so good. Cooks in the Mediterranean know not to mess with a good thing – fish is grilled whole or filleted, meats are prepared simply, cut into thin or small pieces, and both are sometimes marinated and other times not. And all are cooked fast.

LIGHTING AND COOKING WITH CHARCOAL

• To prepare the barbecue, place enough charcoal in the bowl of the barbecue to give you a good, even layer. Don't fill it too full as you will want to leave a section to one side clear of charcoal, so that you can move food away from the flames if they flare up. Now pile the unlit charcoal in the centre and place rolled-up old newspaper, paper bags or kindling among the pile. You can also use firelighters. Ignite the paper or kindling, then using a flexible piece of cardboard, plastic lid or small baking tray to fan the flames. Alternatively, you can pile the charcoal into a grilling chimney, with paper or kindling, and light that. It is important to know that fire needs oxygen, so don't cover the barbecue. Also, if you are lucky enough to have moveable vents in the base of your barbecue, keep them open to allow a flow of air/oxygen to pass through the fire.

• Once the fire gets going, fan a bit more and, when the charcoal starts to look white hot, spread it out over the bowl of the barbecue, remembering to leave a small area to one side. If you use a chimney to light the charcoal, this means you can only light so much at a time, so empty out into the barbecue and spread out to the required space; if you need more, simply pile on a few more coals and leave to burn until white hot.

• Set the grill rack at least 20cm above the charcoal and leave to heat up. Use a silicone brush to brush it with oil and leave to burn off. The grill rack really needs to be hot as this will prevent the food from sticking to it. To check it has reached the correct heat, hover your hand over the charcoal and, if you can feel the heat but hold it there for 3 seconds, it's good. You do not want it to be too hot, nor too cool.

• Place the meat or fish on the rack over the charcoal and listen for that satisfying sizzle the moment it lands on the grill. You don't want the charcoal to flare up too much; if it does, you need to lift up the food and transfer it to the side, where there is no charcoal, until the flames calm down. My father always sprinkles fine salt over the hot charcoal if this happens, as it helps the flames to die down.

• While the food is cooking, keep seasoning and brushing the meat with oil or marinade, and keep turning it regularly. If cooking kebabs, ensure the meat and vegetables are kept slightly separate on the skewers. And there's no need to ever cover the grill – that's only necessary for a whole different style of grilling!

• Cleaning the barbecue is very important and it's best to do straightaway, as otherwise the next time you grill, it becomes a chore. Ideally, as soon as the food is removed from the grill rack, you should brush it with a steel brush. Brush with a little clean oil and then leave to heat until the charcoal cools down. The oil will seal the grill rack and so prevent rusting, which means you will be able to start easily the next time you barbecue.

Mix 'n' match marinades

These marinades are good to use on all meat, poultry and fish. Remember, if marinated in the fridge, give the food enough time (about 30 minutes) to come back to room temperature before cooking.

ZA'ATAR-STYLE

Lightly crush 2 tablespoons toasted sesame seeds using a pestle and mortar with 1 teaspoon cumin seeds. Mix the seeds with 2 tablespoons dried mint, 2 tablespoons dried oregano, 4 tablespoons extra virgin olive oil and the grated zest and juice of 1 lemon. Rub all over the meat/fish and marinate at room temperature for 30 minutes to 2 hours in the fridge. For fish, marinate only at room temperature for 30 minutes.

SERVES 4 138 calories, 0.4g carbs, 14.8g fat, 2.2g sat fat, 1.6g protein

ROSEMARY AND BALSAMIC VINEGAR

Separate 2 large rosemary sprigs into small sprigs and mix with 100ml balsamic vinegar, 150ml extra virgin olive oil, 3 minced garlic cloves and 1 tablespoon clear honey. Season. Rub all over the meat, poultry or fish and marinate the meat and chicken at room temperature for 30 minutes or for 2 hours in the fridge. Fish fillets should be marinated at room temperature for 20 minutes, or for 1 hour in the fridge and 2 hours for whole fish. For mackerel, omit the honey.

SERVES 4 377 calories, 8.9g carbs, 37.5g fat, 5.3g sat fat, 0.5g protein

OREGANO, FENNEL AND CHILLI MARINADE

Bash 2 tablespoons fennel seeds with 1 tablespoon chilli flakes using a pestle and mortar. Add 2 tablespoons dried oregano and 2 minced garlic cloves. Mix with 4 tablespoons extra virgin olive oil and the juice of 1 lemon. Rub all over the meat, poultry or fish; marinate at room temperature or in the fridge for up to 1 hour. For whole fish and fish fillets, marinate for 30 minutes at room temperature and 3 hours in the fridge.

SERVES 4 102 calories, 0.47g carbs, 12g fat, 1.6g sat fat, 1.3g protein

FRESH HERBS AND GARLIC

Simply use whichever fresh herbs are around at the time. Strip the leaves from 2 large rosemary sprigs (or herb of your choice) and roughly chop. Mix with 3 tablespoons extra virgin olive oil, 3 tablespoons red wine vinegar or the juice of 1 lemon. Add 2 minced garlic cloves and season. Marinate for at least 30 minutes at room temperature or 2 hours in the fridge.

SERVES 4 79 calories, 0.5g carbs, 8.2g fat, 1.2g sat fat, 0.25g protein

BARBECUED LAMB SIRLOIN WITH BLACK OLIVES AND PARSLEY

This lamb tastes incredible cooked over a charcoal barbecue. However, you can also sear it on a cast-iron griddle pan for 3 minutes on each side and then finish in a preheated oven at 220°C/425°F/gas mark 7 for a further 5 minutes.

750g lamb sirloin steak (see page 82), trimmed of fat
½ quantity Oregano, Fennel and Chilli Marinade (see left)
2 lemons
110g salt-cured black olives, pitted
25g flat-leaf parsley sprigs
sea salt flakes
extra virgin olive oil, to serve
grain pilaf (see pages 58–59) and chopped salad or grilled
   vegetables, to serve

Open out the lamb steak, place between sheets of parchment paper and bash with a rolling pin to flatten out to about 1.5cm thick. Rub all over with the marinade and leave to marinate at room temperature for an hour or for 24 hours in the fridge.

Prepare the charcoal barbecue and brush the grill rack with oil.

Place the marinated lamb over the hot charcoal, season with sea salt flakes and cook for 5–8 minutes on each side, turning twice. If the charcoal flames, move the meat to the cooler part of the grill and wait for the flames to calm down. The lamb should feel soft when pressed and be cooked to medium-rare in the middle. Transfer to a large chopping board, cover in a tent of foil and allow to rest for 5 minutes.

Meanwhile, remove the rind and pith from the lemons and slice the flesh into discs. Mix with the olives and parsley sprigs.

Slice the lamb against the grain and arrange on a serving platter. Top with the black olive and lemon salad, drizzle with extra virgin olive oil and serve.

SERVES 4 535 calories, 0.7g carbs, 44.2g fat, 17.8g sat fat, 35.5g protein

Bottom left: pan-seared lamb loin chops; bottom centre: 'Frenched' pork rib chops; top right: fresh basil; middle right: grilling lamb rib chops

Grilled Lamb Sirloin with Black Olives and Parsley (recipe on page 85)

LAMB KOFTES

You can make these koftes spicy by adding either Calabrian chilli flakes or Mediterranean Aleppo pepper. Sometimes, in our Greek-Cypriot world, we also make these using minced pork shoulder. To cook, I recommend you barbecue or pan-fry.

500g minced lamb shoulder
2 garlic cloves, finely grated
1 shallot, chopped
3 tablespoons finely chopped flat-leaf parsley
finely grated zest and juice of 1 lemon
1 teaspoon dried mint
½ teaspoon ground coriander
50g fresh breadcrumbs
1 egg, beaten
1 teaspoon hot spice, see introduction (optional)
sea salt and freshly cracked black pepper
extra virgin olive oil, for shallow-frying
Greek or Turkish Chopped Salad (see page 125), Tahini
    Sauce (see page 48) and parsley sprigs, to serve

Prepare the charcoal barbecue, if using. In a large bowl, place the ground lamb and all the remaining ingredients up to and including the hot spice, if using. Use your hands to mix everything together thoroughly and season with salt and pepper.

To taste for seasoning, heat a little oil in a frying pan and cook about 1 teaspoon of the mixture, so you can test to see if your seasoning is right. Adjust if necessary. Shape the mixture into 12–15 oval patties.

If barbecuing, shape the meat directly onto skewers (you should be able to fit three koftes on each). Place the skewers on the grill rack and listen to the sizzle. Cook for 4 minutes, then brush the top with oil, turn over and cook for another 4 minutes. When cooked, the koftes should still be a little pink in the centre.

To pan-fry, heat 2–3 tablespoons extra virgin olive oil in a frying pan and cook the koftes (not on skewers) for 10 minutes, rolling them to brown and cook on all sides.

Serve with a chopped Greek or Turkish salad, drizzle with tahini sauce and scatter with parsley sprigs.

Tip: If the flames flare up, lift the skewers to a cooler part of the barbecue, allow the flames to subside and then return to the hot charcoal to finish cooking. You can also grill these koftes under a preheated grill for 5–6 minutes on each side.

MAKES 12–15, SERVES 4

337 calories, 10.8g carbs, 20.9g fat, 8.5g sat fat, 27.3g protein

Lamb Koftes

Pork Souvlaki

PORK CUTS

• **Pork rib chops** – these generally have a rib bone running along one side and sometimes a layer of fat on the outside. They are sometimes 'Frenched'; this is when the meat is removed from part of the bone. (See page 92 to see how to brine.)

• **Pork loin chop** – often you have meat on either side of the bone, like a T-bone steak, and this is known as a centre-cut pork loin chop. Depending on where they're cut from, these chops will have loin meat on one side and leaner tenderloin meat on the other.

• **Pork shoulder chop** – these are from the shoulder, with a narrow bone in the centre coming from the blade bone. The meat is darker than pork loin chops, plus it's fattier and has connective tissue, which gives it a lot of juicy flavour.

• **Sirloin pork chop** – this cheaper cut contains more bone than other chops and also a mixture of fat and connective tissue (also known as gristle). Good for both quick and slow cooking methods.

• **Pork shoulder** – this meat has very good marbling and, when cut into small 2–3cm cubes, makes the best souvlaki or kebabs (see right).

• **Pork belly steaks** – this boneless fatty meat is very popular these days. My favourite way to eat it is sliced into very thin steaks, sprinkled with salt and local herbs and grilled over charcoal. Ask the butcher to slice it 7mm thick, and the rind can be on or off – it will never be like crackling, so no big deal.

• **Spare rib 'steaks'** – I have had these in Greece, where they cut the ribs crossways, so the steak has three flat rib bones, with lots of flavoursome meat and fat holding them together. They are very thinly sliced, about 5mm, so cooking is super-fast.

PORK SOUVLAKI

This is my absolute favourite – small chunks of pork shoulder, perfect amount of marbling with lots of flavour, simply seasoned with salt. All you then have to do is tuck it into pitta bread with salad and a drizzle of tahini or tzatziki.

675g pork shoulder, cut into 2–3cm chunks
2 teaspoons sea salt flakes, plus extra for sprinkling
2 teaspoons dried marjoram or oregano (optional)
3 tablespoons tahini paste
juice of 1 lemon
2 tablespoons extra virgin olive oil
toasted pitta bread (optional)
Greek or Turkish Chopped Salad, minus the feta
  (see page 125)

Prepare the charcoal barbecue and brush the grill rack with oil.

Mix the pork in a bowl with the salt and dried marjoram or oregano (if using). Thread the pork pieces onto eight metal skewers (do not over-stuff and allow a little space between each piece). Place the skewers onto the grill rack and listen for that sizzle. Cook for 3 minutes on each side (that's four sides), moving the skewers over to the cooler side if the flames start to flare up. Separate the pieces of meat when they seem to be sticking together. On the last turn, sprinkle the souvlaki with a little salt.

Place the tahini in a bowl and whisk in 150ml cold water until the paste turns smooth and runny but still coats the back of a spoon. Season with salt, a squeeze or two of lemon juice and a generous drizzle of extra virgin olive oil, adjusting the flavourings to suit your taste.

To assemble, open out each toasted pitta bread into a pocket, spread either side with some tahini sauce and stuff the base with Greek or Turkish Chopped Salad, then top with a skewer or two of meat. Spoon over more tahini sauce and serve.

SERVES 4 345 calories, 0.2g carbs, 21.4g fat, 4.4g sat fat, 37.9g protein

ROASTED PORK CHOPS WITH BROCCOLI RAPINI

You can vary the flavour combos, adding dried oregano (for sesame) and lemon juice (instead of vinegar) to the chops while cooking, and the vegetable in the pan can be small florets of cauliflower (in place of broccoli rapini). Another combo can be roughly crushed coriander seeds (for sesame), dry or sweet sherry (for vinegar), and parsnips (in place of broccoli rapini).

3 tablespoons extra virgin olive oil
4 brined pork chops (see right), drained and patted dry
8 shallots, halved lengthways
500g broccoli rapini or tenderstem/sprouting broccoli, cut into 7cm pieces
4 tablespoons balsamic vinegar
2 tablespoons toasted sesame seeds
salad and/or pilaf (see pages 58–59), to serve

Preheat the oven to 200°C/400°F/gas mark 6. Heat the olive oil in a large, ovenproof frying pan, add the pork chops and sear on each side over a high heat for 5 minutes, until you get a good even brown colour. Take off the heat and set aside.

Drain the excess fat out of the pan, leaving only about 2 tablespoons. Add the shallots, cut-side down, and the broccoli and sear, turning once, until slightly charred. Transfer to a plate and set aside.

Add the vinegar and deglaze the pan. Return the chops, broccoli and shallots to the pan, add 75ml water and sprinkle with the sesame seeds. Transfer the pan to the oven and cook for 15 minutes. Serve with a fresh salad and/or a pilaf.

SERVES 4 514 calories, 8.1g carbs, 39.9g fat, 12g sat fat, 30.7g protein

HOW TO BARBECUE OR PAN-ROAST PORK CHOPS

Pork chops that are high in fat and connective tissue should be cooked over a high heat first for colour and flavour, and then quite quickly transferred to the cooler side of the barbecue or in the oven where they can cook for a little longer to ensure they are cooked through. Remember, pork chops can be a little pink in the centre – they really do taste better and juicier that way.

Pork rib and loin chops can dry out very easily during cooking and so it's a good idea to brine them first. If each chop is 2–2.5cm thick, it will only need 1 hour of simple brining at room temperature or up to 6 hours in the fridge. The chops should then be drained, wrapped in clingfilm and stored for up to 2 days in the fridge (you can also freeze them for up to 3 months, as long as they have not been frozen before).

FOR A SIMPLE BRINE

Dissolve 50g fine salt and 50g brown sugar in 750ml water in a saucepan over a low heat. Add 10–15 ice cubes to cool the liquid quickly, then add 4 rib pork chops. You can also add more flavourings to your brine to make it like a marinade – 4 rosemary sprigs, 3 bashed garlic cloves, 1 chopped onion or 100ml pomegranate molasses. Continue as per the instructions above.

Roasted Pork Chops with Broccoli Rapini

Whole fish

WHOLE FISH

The method you choose to cook fish depends on the size of the fish or the type of cut and its thickness. When cooking a whole fish, I advise you keep it easy for yourself and choose one that is a manageable size, like branzino (small sea bass), sea bass, red snapper, red mullet, mackerel or sea bream.

Assuming you will serve one whole fish per person, select ones that are 350–450g each and have them gutted, scaled and cleaned by the fishmonger! Use a sharp knife to cut three small slits on each side of the fish and season all over and inside with salt and pepper. Have the barbecue ready with charcoal or preheat the oven to 200°C/400°F/gas mark 6. You can also use the grill to cook all fish cuts.

TO PAN-SEAR

Many people are scared to cook fish in a pan as they are afraid of it sticking. However, as long as the pan is well heated and the fish has been rubbed with oil, it shouldn't stick. Follow these simple rules and it's the easiest method in the world. Flavour is, of course, important so rub the fish with salt and pepper and other seasonings as well as oil, and ensure the fish is at room temperature before you start to cook. Fish fillets or thick cuts should have 2–3 cuts in the skin in order to allow even cooking.

Place a non-stick, stainless steel or cast-iron pan over a high heat. When you think it's hot, flick a little water into it and, if it sizzles and evaporates, you're ready. Turn the heat down, drizzle in a little extra virgin olive oil and swirl to coat the base of the pan. Place the fish, skin-side down, in the hot pan and, pressing down with a flat spatula, cook for 2 minutes as this will ensure a crispy skin. Release the pressure and cook for a further 2 minutes, then flip the fish over and continue to cook for 2 minutes. You should not need to cook any further in the oven. Take the pan off the heat and allow to stand for 3 minutes. Thick cuts of fish (about 5cm) should cook for 2–3 minutes longer, but be careful not to overcook. Remember, fish continues to cook after you take it off the heat and should not be dry, but juicy.

TO BARBECUE OR GRILL

Tuck lemon slices in the cavities of each fish, season well and rub all over with extra virgin olive oil. Prepare the barbecue as per page 84. Place the fish on the grill and you should hopefully hear an immediate sizzle as the skin immediately sears (don't forget to brush the grill rack with oil!). Cook the fish for 5–8 minutes on each side, depending on how thick the fish is. It is ready when the skin is a little charred and blistered and the flesh is just turning opaque. For me, if you see a little pink near the bone, it's a good sign as the fish will continue cooking after it is taken off the grill. Large sea bass and red snapper will take 12–15 minutes on each side. They are heavy, so use two large fish spatulas to flip the fish over. I prefer to roll it, rather than lifting it up – that's too hard!

If you are going to grill, ensure to preheat the grill. If cooking whole fish such as mackerel, large sardines, red mullet or branzino, cut slits on each side, and cook for 10–15 minutes, depending on size. I just cook the fish on one side, I do not turn them over. For small sardines, do not cut slits; cook for 10 minutes on one side. If cooking fillets or cuts of fish, then cook just for 6–8 minutes, skin-side down.

FOR ROASTING

Preheat the oven to 200°C/400°F/gas mark 6. Arrange lemon slices over the base of a shallow baking tray. Cut 2–3 slits on each side of each whole fish, and lay the fish on the lemon slices. Tuck a few more lemon slices into the cavity of each fish with a sprig or two of parsley, thyme or rosemary; finish with a drizzle of extra virgin olive oil (about 1 tablespoon per fish). Roast for 25 minutes until the fish is golden, starting to char in places and the flesh is just turning opaque white. Large whole sea bass and red snapper will take a little longer – up to 40 minutes in the oven. Be careful not to overcook. You do not need to turn the fish over.

Serve the fish with any of the sauces, salsas, gremolata or tapenades on the following pages.

SUNFLOWER SEED GREMOLATA

75g sunflower seeds, toasted
finely grated zest of 1 lemon or orange
½ teaspoon Calabrian chilli flakes
2 tablespoons finely chopped oregano or flat-leaf parsley
sea salt flakes
extra virgin olive oil, to serve

Roughly chop the sunflower seeds and then mix in a bowl with all the remaining dry ingredients. Season with salt to taste. Sprinkle the gremolata over the grilled, seared or roasted fish, drizzle with extra virgin olive oil and serve.

SERVES 4 113 calories, 3.6g carbs, 9.3g fat, 1.3g sat fat, 3.9g protein

OLIVE, CHILLI AND PARSLEY

75g large green olives (Castelvetrano), pitted
1 teaspoon Calabrian chilli flakes
3 tablespoons finely chopped flat-leaf parsley
juice of ½ lemon
4 tablespoons extra virgin olive oil
sea salt and freshly cracked black pepper

Finely chop the green olives and mix in a bowl with the chilli flakes, parsley, lemon juice and olive oil. Taste and season with salt and pepper. Add a little more lemon juice if necessary and serve over your choice of cooked fish.

SERVES 4 119 calories, 0.1g carbs, 13.2g fat, 1.9g sat fat, 0.4g protein

CAPER AND OLIVE SALSA

75g green olives (cracked variety), pitted
50g salted capers, soaked, drained and chopped
½ teaspoon Calabrian chilli flakes (optional)
3 tablespoons finely chopped dill
1 tablespoon finely chopped flat-leaf parsley
4 tablespoons extra virgin olive oil
juice of ½ lemon
sea salt and freshly cracked black pepper

Finely chop the olives and place in a bowl. Mix with all the remaining ingredients and taste for seasoning. Serve over your choice of cooked fish.

SERVES 4 122 calories, 0.8g carbs, 13.2g fat, 71.9g sat fat, 0.6g protein

FENNEL AND PARSLEY SALSA

1 small bulb of fennel or 2 small bulbs of wild fennel
juice of 1 lemon
6 tablespoons extra virgin olive oil
3 tablespoons finely chopped flat-leaf parsley
sea salt and freshly cracked black pepper

Trim and finely chop the fennel and then place in a bowl with the lemon juice. Leave to stand for 10 minutes until the fennel has softened slightly. Stir in the olive oil and parsley, taste for seasoning and serve over your choice of cooked fish.

SERVES 4 154 calories, 0.8g carbs, 16.6g fat, 2.4g sat fat, 0.5g protein

TOMATO, FENNEL AND BLACK OLIVE

4 tablespoons extra virgin olive oil
2 small bulbs of fennel, trimmed and thinly sliced
250g ripe cherry tomatoes
75g Kalamata olives, pitted and halved
2 tablespoons red wine vinegar
sea salt and freshly cracked black pepper

Heat half the oil in a medium frying pan and add the fennel. Cook for 3–5 minutes until wilted and then add the tomatoes. Cook for 5 minutes until the tomatoes burst. Stir in the olives and vinegar and heat through. Season to taste, stir in the remaining oil and serve over your choice of cooked fish.

SERVES 4 143 calories, 3.6g carbs, 13.5g fat, 2g sat fat, 1.6g protein

CLASSIC LEMON AND OLIVE OIL DRESSING

2 lemon halves
6–8 tablespoons extra virgin olive oil
2 tablespoons finely chopped flat-leaf parsley
sea salt and freshly cracked black pepper

To get extra juice from the lemons, grill or sear the lemon halves over a high heat for 1 minute, cut-side down. Squeeze the juice into a bowl and mix with the oil. Add the parsley, stir in 1 tablespoon water and season to taste. Serve over your choice of cooked fish.

SERVES 4 150 calories, 0.2g carbs, 16.5 fat, 2.4g sat fat, 0.1g protein

YOGURT AND PRESERVED LEMONS

1 large preserved lemon or 2 small, rinsed and chopped
150ml thick Greek yogurt
6 tablespoons extra virgin olive oil
3 tablespoons finely chopped mint or flat-leaf parsley
sea salt and freshly cracked black pepper

There is a huge variety of preserved lemons on the market and some are much stronger in flavour than others. For very salty large preserved lemons, cut in half, scoop out the centre and discard and then finely dice the rind. For the smaller variety, wash, pat dry and finely chop the whole lemon.

In a bowl, mix the lemon with the yogurt, olive oil and herbs. Taste, adjust the seasoning and serve over your choice of fish. Finish with a little more drizzled olive oil and herb leaves, if liked.

SERVES 4 202 calories, 2.4g carbs, 20.4g fat, 4.9g sat fat, 2.4g protein

PISTACHIO, SESAME AND BLACK OLIVES

1 whole lemon
2 tablespoons roasted chopped pistachios
2 tablespoons toasted sesame seeds
2 tablespoons finely chopped oil-cured black olives
4 tablespoons extra virgin olive oil

Using a sharp knife, remove the rind and pith from the lemon and cut between the membranes to make segments. Place in a bowl and gently toss with the pistachios, sesame seeds and olives. Mix together with the olive oil and serve over your choice of cooked fish.

SERVES 4 175 calories, 0.9g carbs, 18.1g fat, 2.7g sat fat, 2.2g protein

Pan-Roasted Halibut with Capers

PAN-ROASTING MEAT, POULTRY AND FISH

My favourite way to cook fish or cuts of meat and poultry is to pan-roast, which means you start in an ovenproof frying pan and finish in a hot 200°C/400°F/gas mark 6 oven for the final 10–20 minutes, depending on the thickness of the fillet or cut.

With fish – For fillets at least 2.5cm thick. First cut 2–3 slits in the skin of the fish to prevent curling and to allow for even heat distribution. Rub all over with extra virgin olive oil and season with salt and freshly cracked black pepper. Place in a ovenproof frying pan (the handle determines this – all metal is good, a rubber handle might be okay, but read the instructions, and a wooden handle is a no). Start cooking the fish, skin-side down, for 2–3 minutes, pressing down so that the skin turns crispy and golden. Turn the fish, add any other components, be it a splash of wine, lemon juice or vegetables, and continue to cook until the liquid bubbles. Transfer the pan to the oven and cook for a further 5–10 minutes depending on the thickness of the fillet or fish. Fish steaks (e.g. horseshoe-shaped salmon, cod or swordfish with skin around the outside of the cut) are seared on the two flesh sides.

With meat and poultry – This follows the same procedure. Brown the chops, steak or poultry pieces in a little oil in the heatproof frying pan for 5–8 minutes to achieve a good even colour. Remove the meat and set aside to drain. Add vegetables and other flavourings to the pan and cook, then remove with a slotted spoon and set aside. Deglaze the pan with wine, citrus juice, vinegar or stock. Return all the ingredients to the pan, bring to a bubble and then transfer to the oven until cooked through – 10–20 minutes, but the amount of time depends on the thickness of the cut and your preferred finish.

PAN-ROASTED HALIBUT WITH CAPERS

You can use any salmon, swordfish, cod or tuna for this recipe, as capers, fennel, celery and lemon juice are great accompanying flavours for just about all fish. If using tuna, remember it only needs to be seared for a very short amount of time, as you don't want to overcook and ruin a fine-quality cut.

3 tablespoons extra virgin olive oil
3 tablespoons salted capers, soaked and drained
2 small bulbs of fennel, trimmed and cut into wedges
2 x 175g halibut fillets, about 2.5cm thick, or fish of choice
4–6 celery sticks with leaves
juice of 1 lemon
sea salt and freshly cracked black pepper
extra virgin olive oil, to serve
grain pilaf (see pages 58–59) or chopped or seasonal salad,
　to serve

Preheat the oven to 200°C/400°F/gas mark 6.

Heat the oil in an ovenproof frying pan, add the capers and cook over a high heat until they start to pop open. Remove with a slotted spoon and drain on kitchen paper.

Add the fennel to the pan juices and cook for 5 minutes until caramelised on both sides. Set aside with the capers.

Season the fish, add to the pan, skin-side down, and cook for 2–3 minutes until the skin is golden brown. Flip the fish over, return the fennel to the pan together with the celery leaves and capers and drizzle over the lemon juice. Once bubbling, transfer the pan to the oven and cook for 10 minutes until the fish is tender and just firm to the touch.

Remove the fish from the pan and allow to cool for 3 minutes. Serve the fish with the fennel mixture spooned over the top.

SERVES 2 387 calories, 8.8g carbs, 20.5g fat, 3.1g sat fat, 40.5g protein

Barbecued Squid and Lemon Salad (recipe on page 104)

BARBECUED SQUID AND LEMON SALAD

You could also serve the barbecued squid with a salad of chopped lemons, shaved fennel, fennel pollen, cucumber and crushed fennel seeds.

750g squid, cleaned and with tentacles and
    bodies separated
6 tablespoons extra virgin olive oil
3 lemons
1 teaspoon fine salt
8–12 spring onions, trimmed
1 teaspoon fennel or cumin seeds, lightly crushed
200g mixed salad leaves, such as radicchio, rocket,
    amaranth and young dandelion leaves
2 large Brandywine heritage tomatoes, sliced
sea salt and freshly cracked black pepper

Prepare the charcoal barbecue (see page 84). Place a cooling rack over the barbecue grill and brush with oil.

Separate the tentacles from the bodies of the squid and cut the latter to open out flat. Place in a bowl and dress with 2 tablespoons of the olive oil, the juice of 1 lemon and a sprinkling of the salt. Add the tentacles and stir once more. Set aside to marinate at room temperature for 30 minutes.

Arrange the squid bodies on the hot grill. Place a piece of foil over the top and then press down with a heavy, cast-iron frying pan or baking tray; this will help the squid to lie flat and cook evenly. Cook for 3–5 minutes. Carefully remove the weight and foil and, using tongs, flip over the squid. Weigh down again and cook for another 3 minutes. Remove the weight and add the squid tentacles and spring onions. Cook for a further 2–3 minutes until the tentacles curl and the spring onions blacken slightly. When done, take everything off the heat and set aside.

Slice the two remaining lemons, brush with oil and grill over the hot charcoal until browned. Remove and, when cool enough to handle, chop, including the rind, and place in a large bowl.

Slice the squid bodies into slices (if they have curled slightly that is all fine). Halve the larger tentacles, or leave whole – it's up to you. Add to the bowl of lemons, stir in the fennel or cumin seeds and another 2 tablespoons of extra virgin olive oil. Season to taste with salt and pepper, then add the salad leaves and toss once more.

To assemble, arrange the sliced tomatoes on four serving plates or on a large platter. Top with the dressed salad and grilled spring onions. Spoon over any salad dressing left in the bowl, drizzle each with a little more extra virgin olive oil and serve.

SERVES 4 333 calories, 6.5g carbs, 20.4g fat, 3.2 sat fat, 32.1g protein

BARBECUED OCTOPUS WITH BABY POTATOES

Here, the octopus is being cooked for that charcoal flavour, as it has already been braised (see page 184). The potatoes can be completed in a frying pan or roasted in a hot oven.

500g Charlotte or new potatoes, scrubbed clean
1 tablespoon coriander seeds, lightly crushed
juice of 2 lemons, plus extra wedges to serve
6 tablespoons extra virgin olive oil
2 small shallots, sliced on a mandolin
1kg Braised Octopus (see page 184), tentacles cut into
  7.5cm pieces
50g baby rocket or baby spinach
sea salt flakes and freshly cracked black pepper

Prepare the charcoal barbecue (see page 84). Place a cooling rack over the barbecue grill and brush with oil.

Meanwhile, place the potatoes in a pan of boiling salted water and bring to the boil. Reduce the heat slightly and cook for 15–20 minutes until tender. Drain.

Once cool enough to handle, gently smash each potato with a fork and place in a bowl with the coriander seeds, finely grated zest and juice of 1 lemon and half the olive oil. Season with salt and pepper.

Place the shallots in a clean bowl with the juice of half the remaining lemon and set aside.

Brush the grill rack with oil once more, leave for a few minutes and then arrange the smashed potatoes on top. Grill for 3–5 minutes on each side, until crisp and toasted.

Meanwhile, mix the remaining oil with the juice of the remaining lemon. Brush this over the octopus and place on the grill or thread onto metal skewers. Cook on each side for 3 minutes, sprinkling with sea salt flakes.

Arrange the potatoes on a large platter, scatter with rocket and add the octopus on top. Drain the shallots and scatter over the octopus. Serve with extra lemon wedges on the side.

SERVES 4 488 calories, 23.1g carbs, 26.1g fat, 4g sat fat, 42.1g protein

GRILLED WHOLE MACKEREL

Cooking a fish whole means that it remains juicy and 'clean-flavoured'. If your guests find eating a whole fish a little daunting, follow the simple instructions below on how to fillet.

4 x 350g whole mackerel, cleaned and trimmed
4 tablespoons extra virgin olive oil
½ teaspoon chilli flakes
2 lemons, finely sliced
8 flat-leaf parsley sprigs
handful of long chives or 4 spring onions
sea salt and freshly cracked black pepper
Fennel and parsley (see page 97) salsa, or any dressing or
  tapenade on pages 96–99, to serve
grain pilaf, to serve (see pages 58-59)

Preheat the oven grill to hot.

Use a sharp knife to cut three small slits on each side of each fish, rub all over with oil and season inside and out with salt and pepper and a sprinkle of chilli flakes. Tuck half the lemon slices inside the fish cavities, add two parsley sprigs in each, plus some chives or a spring onion.

Drizzle a steel or heatproof metal plate with oil. Arrange two prepared fish on each plate, place under the hot grill and cook for 8–12 minutes. Do not flip the fish over. The fish will blister and char in places and the eyes on the fish head will turn opaque. Remove from the heat and gently ease off the plate to a chopping board. Leave to stand for 3 minutes.

To fillet, run a small sharp knife along the outside curve of each fish, from head to tail. Run it along the top and then under the bone and lift the curved bone off. Take a flat metal spatula and gently lift up half the fish, off the central bone, and flip over, to expose the inside of the fish. Gently take out the central bone, lifting from just under the head down to the tail. Remove the few loose bones near the collar of the fish. You can serve or discard the head. Place the fish fillets on a platter, dress and serve.

SERVES 4 572 calories, 1.1g carbs, 47g fat, 9.3g sat fat, 36.5g protein

SWORDFISH KEBABS

Choose an oily fish or firm white fish that has quite a dense texture. Oily fish, such as swordfish, is a classic, as are salmon and tuna. For firm white fish, choose thick fillets of cod and halibut. Also, I prefer to use metal over bamboo skewers. I find the latter tend to dry the food on cooking.

3 tablespoons extra virgin olive oil
750g swordfish, thick skin removed
1 quantity Oregano, Fennel and Chilli Marinade
   (see page 85)
8 small red onions
1 quantity Tahini Sauce (see page 48) or Lemon and Oil
   Dressing (see page 98)
grain pilaf (see pages 58–59), chopped salad or seasonal
   salad, to serve

Preheat the charcoal barbecue to medium-hot (see page 84). Place a cooling rack over the barbecue grill. Brush with oil and leave to heat up.

Cut the swordfish into 3–4cm pieces. Place in a bowl and mix with half the marinade. Cover and leave to stand at room temperature for 30 minutes.

Meanwhile, peel the onions, cut into quarters or eighths, depending on their size. Bring a small pan of water to the boil, add the onions and blanch for 1 minute. Drain and place in a bowl of ice-cold water to cool. Drain.

To assemble, for each skewer, allow six pieces of fish to four pieces of red onion. Start with a wedge of onion, then two pieces of fish, onion, two pieces of fish, onion, two more pieces of fish and finally onion. Make eight skewers in total. Brush the skewers with some of the remaining marinade, and place on the preheated grill rack. Barbecue for 2 minutes, turn, brush with oil and cook for another 2 minutes. Continue twice more, finally brushing with the remaining marinade.

Serve the kebabs with the tahini or the lemon and oil dressing. Serve with a pilaf, chopped salad or seasonal salad.

SERVES 4 541 kcal, 10.3g carbs, 43.1g fat, 6.6g sat fat, 31.8g protein

BARBECUED TUNA, CUCUMBER AND RADISH SALAD

As an alternative to the charcoal grill, you can either sear the fish on a preheated grill pan or a cast-iron pan, searing for 3 minutes on each side. This method will blacken the fish on the outside, which surprisingly the charcoal barbecue does not!

2 x 200g tuna steaks
4 tablespoons extra virgin olive oil
8–12 radishes, depending on size, scrubbed clean
2 small Persian cucumbers, trimmed
25g small flat-leaf parsley sprigs
sea salt and freshly cracked black pepper
1 quantity Caper and Olive Salsa (see page 97)

Prepare the charcoal barbecue and brush the grill rack with oil.

Rub the tuna steaks (ensuring they are at room temperature) with about 1 tablespoon of the oil and season all over. Place on the grill rack and listen to it sizzle. Char-grill for only 3 minutes on each side (it is best served medium-cooked). Take off the heat and set aside to stand for 3 minutes.

Meanwhile, using a mandolin, thinly slice the radishes and cucumbers and place in a large bowl. Add the parsley sprigs, season with salt and pepper and toss together with the remaining extra virgin olive oil.

Divide the salad between four serving plates. Slice the tuna, against the grain, and arrange over the top. Spoon over the tapenade and serve.

SERVES 4 342 calories, 1.9g carbs, 25.6g fat, 3.8g sat fat, 26.7g protein

Barbecued Tuna, Cucumber and Radish Salad

Fish and shellfish are an excellent source of omega-3 fatty acids (EPA and DHA), which have anti-inflammatory and anti-clotting properties.

MUSSELS WITH NDUJA AND TOMATOES

Nduja is a spreadable spicy sausage from Calabria, Italy. It will melt into the sauce and add a spicy kick to the final flavour. Alternatively, you can use three salt-cured anchovies, filleted and washed. It won't taste equivalent, but it's also delicious.

4 tablespoons extra virgin olive oil
100g nduja, skin removed
500g ripe plum tomatoes, skinned and cut into
  large chunks
1 teaspoon fennel seeds, lightly crushed
1.5kg mussels, soaked for 10 minutes to remove any grit
sea salt and freshly cracked black pepper
crusty bread, to serve

Heat half the oil in a sauté pan with a lid. When hot, add the nduja to the pan and gently press into the oil, stirring and pressing into the pan to break it up. Add the tomatoes to the pan with the fennel seeds, cover and cook until broken down, about 10 minutes.

Lift the mussels out of their soaking water and rinse. Add the mussels to the pan and season with salt, then cover again and cook for 8–10 minutes, shaking the pan occasionally. Check to see if the mussels have started to open, stir and cook a little longer until they have all opened.

Taste, adjust the seasoning and serve immediately with crusty bread.

SERVES 4 411 calories, 13.9g carbs, 18.9g fat, 3.3g sat fat, 47.8g protein

PAN-SEARED PRAWNS WITH LEMON AND GARLIC

If you like, flavour the oil with rosemary sprigs (omitting the garlic) and replace the dill with flat-leaf parsley at the end.

3 tablespoons extra virgin olive oil
2 garlic cloves, bashed to split the skins
1 large lemon, thinly sliced
500g raw unpeeled medium-large prawns
½ teaspoon Calabrian chilli flakes
1–2 tablespoons finely chopped dill
sea salt and freshly cracked black pepper
toasted crusty bread or cooked pasta, to serve

Place the oil in a large frying pan with the garlic over a medium heat. When the garlic is sizzling, remove and discard. Add the lemon slices to the oil and cook over a gentle heat until caramelised, then remove and set aside.

Add the prawns to the pan, turn up the heat and season with salt, pepper and the chilli flakes. Cook for 5–8 minutes until the prawns are bright pink and slightly caramelised in places. Return the lemon slices to the pan and stir in the dill. Serve immediately with crusty bread or pasta.

SERVES 4 176 calories, 0.9g carbs, 9.2g fat, 1.4g sat fat, 22.5g protein

Pan-seared Prawns with Lemon and Garlic

Shellfish in Parcels with Mixed Herbs

FISH AND SHELLFISH IN PARCELS

The French and Italians both like to cook food in a pouch or parcel made from parchment paper or foil. The French call it 'en papillote' and the Italians say 'cartoccio'. Whether on the barbecue or in the oven, the food cooks in its own steam and so results in a very moist and lightly cooked dish. It's important to allow plenty of space in each parcel for the air to circulate evenly around the food while cooking.

FOR EACH PARCEL:
175g red snapper, sea bass, mackerel or salmon (about 1.5cm thick) – keep the skin on

OR

175g tuna, salmon, swordfish or halibut steak – these dense, meatier cuts of fish will need longer cooking

OR

250g shellfish such as cockles, mussels and prawns (all with shells on)

PLUS
1 tablespoon extra virgin olive oil
2 tablespoons lemon juice or a splash of dry white wine
sea salt and freshly cracked black pepper

Use any of these parcel fillers (quantities are per parcel):
(FYI – Wild salmon was used in the testing of these parcels.)

MIXED HERBS
3 flat-leaf parsley sprigs
1 large rosemary or thyme sprig
3 spring onions, finely chopped
SERVES 1 423 calories, 1.6g carbs, 28.9g fat, 5.3g sat fat, 39.6g protein

GREEN OLIVES AND LEMONS
50g cracked green olives, pitted
2 slices of lemon
25g baby spinach
SERVES 1 470 calories, 0.5g carbs, 34.3g fat, 6.1g sat fat, 40g protein

FENNEL, TOMATOES AND BLACK OLIVES
50g shaved fennel
6 cherry tomatoes, halved
6 black salt-cured olives, pitted
SERVES 1 452 calories, 3.5g carbs, 31.1g fat, 5.6g sat fat, 40.1g protein

Take a large 30cm square of parchment paper. On one side, place one of the parcel fillers of your choice, season well with salt and pepper and drizzle with a little oil and lemon juice or wine. Lay the fish or shellfish on top, drizzle over the remaining oil and lemon juice. Fold the paper up and over the filling and pinch all the way round to secure, tucking the corners under a couple of times to ensure the parcel is thoroughly sealed. If you are to barbecue these parcels, wrap a sheet of foil around the parcel too, taking care not to squash it and to keep plenty of space inside for the air to circulate.

If barbecuing, ensure the charcoal grill is medium hot – your hand hovering over the charcoal should be comfortable for about 5 seconds. Place the parcels on the grill rack and cook for 3–4 minutes until you start to hear the juices bubbling away. Continue to cook for another 5 minutes (for large pieces of fish, 8 minutes). You can place the lid over the barbecue if you are cooking en papillote. Take off the heat and set aside, unopened, for 5 minutes.

To cook in the oven, place the parcels on a baking tray in a preheated oven at 200°C/400°F/gas mark 6 and cook for 20 minutes. The parchment should puff up and slightly brown. Take out one parcel and open to check the fish is just flaky, or that the mussels or clams have opened, or that the prawns are bright pink. Remember, it will continue to cook once out of the oven. Allow to stand for 3–5 minutes. Serve with crusty bread to mop up the juices.

CHICKEN SOUVLAKI

I don't understand why people choose chicken breast to make kebabs as they're always dry.

My mum makes the best chicken souvlaki, sometimes with a little Chinese barbecue sauce and soy, but here I will stay more authentic. However, she does always thread them onto metal skewers to ensure they are cooked through. (In my Greek world, we never use wooden skewers as we find that it dries out the meat.)

8–12 chicken thighs, boned and skinned
juice of 1 lemon
4 tablespoons extra virgin olive oil
2 tablespoons dried oregano
sea salt and freshly cracked black pepper
chopped tomatoes mixed with flat-leaf parsley, to serve
flatbread, to serve (optional)

FOR THE TZATZIKI
½ cucumber, peeled
100ml Greek yogurt
½ teaspoon dried mint
1 tablespoon extra virgin olive oil
sea salt flakes

Trim the chicken of any sinew and then cut into 4cm-long pieces, about 2.5cm thick. Place in a bowl and mix with the lemon juice, olive oil and oregano. Leave to marinate at room temperature for at least 1 hour, or you can marinate it in the fridge overnight, if you like.

Using two long metal skewer, per ten pieces of chicken, straddle the meat pieces between the two skewers, piercing at each end, as if the skewers were attached at the end, to be double-pronged. Repeat with two more skewers and the remaining chicken. This method of skewering means the chicken will cook evenly.

Preheat the barbecue until it is very hot. If using charcoal, it should be white hot and you should be able to hover your hand over the heat for only a few seconds. Straddle the skewers over the grill rack and cook for 12–15 minutes, turning every 3–5 minutes and seasoning between each turn. When ready, the meat should be tender and evenly charred and caramelised.

Alternatively, cook the skewers under a conventional oven grill or in a really hot oven for 15–20 minutes, turning several times and seasoning as above.

Meanwhile, make the tzatziki. Slice the cucumber lengthways and, using a spoon, scoop out the seeds and discard. Grate the cucumber on a large shred and drain on kitchen paper. Transfer to a bowl, season well and fold in the yogurt with the mint and oil. Season to taste with salt and set aside at room temperature until ready to serve.

To serve, remove the chicken from the skewers and serve with the tzatziki and chopped tomato salad. Serve with flatbread too, if you like.

SERVES 6 271 calories, 1.2g carbs, 18.8g fat, 4.6g sat fat, 24.4g protein

PAN-SEARED CHICKEN THIGHS WITH CAPERS AND PARSLEY

The ideal way to serve these crispy chicken thighs is with a small Greek Salad on the side (see page 125), or with Roasted Greens (see page 148) or a wholegrain pilaf (see pages 58–59).

8 boned chicken thighs, with skin still intact
2 tablespoons extra virgin olive oil
2 shallots, finely chopped
2 tablespoons salted capers, soaked and drained
splash of lemon juice or Marsala wine (depending on your taste – tart with lemon juice, or slightly sweet with Marsala wine)
15g flat-leaf parsley sprigs, finely chopped
sea salt and freshly cracked black pepper
Turkish Chopped Salad (see page 125) or grain pilaf (see pages 58–59), to serve

Trim the chicken pieces of fat and open out. Season well with salt and freshly cracked black pepper and rub all over with a little of the oil. Place a large cast-iron pan over a high heat and sear the chicken, skin-side down, for 5–8 minutes for the fat to render out.

Drain all but 2 tablespoons of fat from the pan and flip the chicken over. Add the shallots, reduce the heat and cook slowly until soft and the chicken is almost cooked through (25 minutes in total). Stir in the capers and add the lemon juice or marsala wine. Allow to bubble up for a minute and then stir in the parsley. Serve immediately with a salad or pilaf of your choice.

SERVES 4 345 calories, 1g carbs, 25.9g fat, 6.4g sat fat, 27.2g protein

CHICKEN THIGHS WITH FENNEL, BLACK OLIVES AND BLOOD ORANGES

Blood oranges are very seasonal and available in the winter months. Use a tart-flavoured orange if blood oranges are not in season.

8 boned chicken thighs, trimmed with skin still intact
6 tablespoons red wine vinegar
4 tablespoons extra virgin olive oil
2 garlic cloves, bashed to split the skins
2–3 fennel bulbs, trimmed and thinly sliced
75g pitted black olives
4 blood oranges, peeled of skin and pith, then sliced into discs
15g chopped fennel fronds or dill
sea salt and freshly cracked black pepper

Arrange the chicken in a single layer in a large shallow dish. Pour over half the red wine vinegar and half the oil and season well. Marinate at room temperature for 30 minutes.

Place a large cast-iron pan over a high heat and sear the chicken, skin-side down, pressing down with another heavy pan, until the skin is quite crisp and the fat has rendered off, about 8 minutes. Turn the meat over and continue to cook until tender – about 25 minutes in total. Remove from the pan and allow to stand for 10 minutes, draining on kitchen paper.

Meanwhile, heat the remaining oil in a large frying pan and add the garlic cloves. Cook for 3 minutes and then remove and discard the garlic. Add the fennel to the oil and fry in a single layer for 3 minutes on each side, until golden brown. Remove with a slotted spoon and drain on kitchen paper.

Add the olives to the pan and cook for 3 minutes, then add the remaining red wine vinegar and allow to sizzle.

To assemble, arrange the chicken thighs, crispy fennel and blood orange slices on a large serving platter. Spoon over the black olive dressing, sprinkle with fennel fronds or dill and serve.

SERVES 4 396 calories, 7.7g carbs, 29.8g fat, 6.3g sat fat, 23.6g protein

Chicken Thighs with Fennel, Black Olives, and Blood Oranges (recipe on page 115)

BARBECUED CHICKEN WITH GREEN OLIVES

If you do not want to joint your own chicken, the butcher will do this for you, or simply use thigh and drumstick pieces. I think the brown meat on the bone is perfect for barbecues as it delivers the best, juiciest results. If barbecuing chicken breast, ensure that it is still on the bone, with the skin intact too.

1 whole chicken, jointed into 8 pieces
1 quantity Oregano, Fennel and Chilli Marinade (page 85)
4 tablespoons extra virgin olive oil
juice and finely grated zest of 2 lemons
200g salt-cured anchovies, filleted (see page 34), optional
200g large green olives, pitted and halved
15g finely chopped flat-leaf parsley
15g finely chopped mint
sea salt and freshly cracked black pepper
grain pilaf (see pages 58–59) and roasted or grilled
  vegetables (see pages 142–152), to serve

In a shallow dish, turn and coat the chicken in the marinade and set aside at room temperature to marinate for at least 45 minutes.

Prepare the charcoal grill until hot (see page 84) and brush the grill rack with oil. If you would rather roast the chicken, preheat the oven to 220°C/425°F/gas mark 7.

Place the chicken on the grill and listen to it sizzle as the skin instantly sears. If the flames flare up, move the meat over to the cooler side until they subside. Cook the chicken for about 25 minutes, turning regularly and seasoning and brushing with a little of the marinade. To cook in the oven, place the chicken on a rack over a baking tray and roast for 35 minutes, turning and brushing with some of the marinade halfway through.

In a bowl, mix the olive oil and lemon zest and juice. Mash the anchovies, if using, and add to the dressing with the olives, parsley and mint. Taste for seasoning, and adjust if needed. Arrange the cooked chicken on a platter and spoon over the dressing. Serve with a pilaf and vegetables.

SERVES 6 488 calories, 0.6g carbs, 40.5g fat, 8.8g sat fat, 32.3g protein

PAN-ROASTED CHICKEN WITH SESAME AND ESCAROLE

When I was a schoolgirl, my mum would telephone me from work and tell me to start preparing the evening meal. For our grilled chicken dinners, I had to cut a whole bird into pieces, and at first I had no idea what to do as I was never taught, I was just expected to do it. And so I'd pull on the rubber washing-up gloves (I didn't like touching the raw meat) and cut away at all the joints that made sense. Depending on how I was feeling, there were sometimes six or eight pieces, sometimes 12!

1 whole chicken, jointed into 8 pieces
4 tablespoons extra virgin olive oil
8 shallots, halved lengthways
2 tablespoons toasted sesame seeds
1 head of escarole or broad-leaved endive
sea salt and freshly cracked black pepper
grain pilaf (see pages 58–59), to serve

Preheat the oven to 200°C/400°F/gas mark 6.

Rub the chicken pieces all over with half the oil and season with salt and pepper. Heat the remaining oil in a large, ovenproof sauté pan over a high heat and sear the chicken all over, about 10 minutes. Drain off all but 2 tablespoons of the fat.

Add the shallots to the chicken in the pan, cut-side down, sprinkle over the sesame seeds and transfer to the oven to roast for 20 minutes.

Meanwhile, wash and dry the escarole or endive, picking the leaves apart. Roughly tear or cut the leaves to about 7.5cm long. Tuck the leaves under and over the chicken in the pan, and return to the oven. Roast for a further 10 minutes until the chicken is very tender and the greens have wilted. Serve with a pilaf of your choice.

SERVES 4 641 calories, 2.3g carbs, 48.4g fat, 11.6g sat fat, 49g protein

Pan-roasted Chicken with Sesame and Escarole

A SALAD AND MORE

This chapter includes salads, roasting and grilling/ barbecuing vegetables. One method can work for a variety of ingredients; it just depends on the season and the amount of time you have on your hands. Salads can be served as a simple starter or, with the addition of a quick grilled or pan-seared protein, make a very satisfying main course for lunch or dinner. With Mediterranean salads, there are no creamy mayonnaise-based dressings. Almost all are dressed with a mere drizzle of extra virgin olive oil and lemon juice or vinegar. I like to roast vegetables as I find it easier to spread large amounts of greens, squashes and root vegetables on large baking trays, than squashing them in a frying pan. Or, if I am barbecuing meat, poultry or fish, I will just adapt my vegetable recipe so I can barbecue the veg on there too. I also like the idea of carpaccio of vegetables! Although the term carpaccio was first used to serve raw thin pieces of fish and meat, it also seems a perfect idea for serving young tender vegetables in season. The vegetables are thinly sliced, often on a mandolin, topped with a pungent or salty cheese, drizzled with extra virgin olive oil, and maybe the odd seed or nut is added, then served. It's a perfect appetiser or side salad.

Chopped salads

RADICCHIO AND PARSLEY SALAD

Teaming up the slightly bitter radicchio leaf with a sweet herb is the perfect match. Serve with grilled or roasted fish, meat and poultry.

1 small (225g) head of radicchio
110g rocket
50g flat-leaf parsley, large stalks removed
2 tablespoons red wine vinegar
3 tablespoons extra virgin olive oil
50g finely grated Parmesan or pecorino
sea salt and freshly cracked black pepper

Finely shred the salad leaves and the parsley. Toss to mix and then dress with the vinegar and oil and toss again. Fold in the Parmesan or pecorino, season to taste and serve.

SERVES 6 96 calories, 0.7g carbs, 8.2g fat, 2.4g sat fat, 4.6g protein

BROAD BEAN AND PECORINO SALAD

Early summer broad beans are sweet and perfect eaten raw, straight from their pods. As the season moves on, you will need to quickly blanch them in boiling water and then remove the thick outer skins – it's worth it.

1kg broad beans in their pods, podded
juice of 1 lemon
4 tablespoons extra virgin olive oil
3 Little Gem lettuces, leaves separated and shredded
50g pecorino, shaved (or grated on a microplane)
sea salt and freshly cracked black pepper

Place the broad beans in a large bowl and mix with the lemon juice, olive oil and seasoning. Toss in the lettuce leaves and then serve on plates with a scattering of cheese on top.

SERVES 6 163 calories, 7.8g carbs, 10.8g fat, 2.8g sat fat, 9.1g protein

DANDELION AND CUCUMBER SALAD

If dandelions are unavailable, use another bitter leaf like rocket, watercress or chicory. This salad is delicious served with barbecued, grilled or roasted fish, meat and poultry.

50g young dandelion leaves, finely shredded
200g cucumber, chopped
juice of 1 lemon
3 tablespoons extra virgin olive oil
100g halloumi, coarsely grated
sea salt and freshly cracked black pepper

Into a large bowl, put the dandelion leaves and toss in the chopped cucumber with the lemon juice and oil. Gently fold in the halloumi, season to taste and serve.

SERVES 6 111 calories, 0.7g carbs, 9.7g fat, 3.6g sat fat, 5.2g protein

FENNEL AND HAZELNUT SALAD

For this salad, you could also shave the fennel instead of grating it. Spread out on a large flat platter, then top with the pecorino and hazelnuts for a 'carpaccio-style' salad.

2–4 young fennel bulbs, or 2 medium-sized bulbs, trimmed
juice of 1 lemon
3–4 tablespoons extra virgin olive oil
30g pecorino, shaved
30g toasted hazelnuts (can be salted)
sea salt and freshly cracked black pepper

Coarsely grate the fennel into a large bowl, drizzle with the lemon juice and olive oil and season with salt and pepper. Toss well and then set aside for 10 minutes.

Mix in the shaved pecorino and hazelnuts and then taste, adjust the seasoning if necessary, and serve.

SERVES 4 166 calories, 2.4g carbs, 15.4g fat, 3g sat fat, 4.7g protein

Radicchio and Parsley Salad; Dandelion and Cucumber Salad

Village Greek Salad

VILLAGE GREEK SALAD

A Greek salad, which is served at almost every meal, varies from one island to the next and from one family to the other. My parents are from Cyprus and so our version is influenced by the East and uses coriander and crunchy cabbage. However, it doesn't include feta, as for some reason my mother's side of the family do not have this tradition. My mother and other relatives cut the ingredients very small, whereas my father's side of the family keep their ingredients on the larger side. All is correct as it's the final flavour that counts. On a recent visit to Tinos, the salad there included only cucumber, tomato, red onion and Manouri, a local type of ricotta, and black olives, but it was the perfect taste of where we were.

4 ripe tomatoes
2 small Lebanese cucumbers (200g)
100g romaine or rocket or purslane (depending
  on the season)
2 tablespoons red wine vinegar
3 tablespoons extra virgin olive oil, plus extra to serve
100g feta, thinly sliced
6 black olives
½ red onion, sliced into rings
pinch of dried mint or oregano
sea salt and freshly cracked black pepper

Roughly chop the tomatoes, cucumbers and salad greens and place in a large bowl. Toss with the vinegar and oil and season to taste. Top with the feta, olives and red onion, then sprinkle with a little dried mint or oregano. Drizzle with an extra splash of extra virgin olive oil and serve.

SERVES 6 116 calories, 3.4g carbs, 9.6g fat, 3.2g sat fat, 4g protein

TURKISH CHOPPED SALAD

I always think of this Turkish salad as a Greek-ish Cypriot salad, as they are very similar. The cabbage lends it a delicious crunch. It's excellent served with grilled meats, poultry and fish.

200g red or white cabbage, shredded
juice of 1 lemon
3 tablespoons extra virgin olive oil
2 Lebanese cucumbers (200g)
2 large ripe tomatoes
1 small red onion
15g flat-leaf parsley
15g fresh coriander
sea salt and freshly cracked black pepper

Place the cabbage in a large bowl, toss with the lemon juice and olive oil and set aside for 10 minutes for the cabbage to soften slightly.

Roughly chop all the remaining ingredients, add to the bowl and toss with the cabbage. Season to taste and serve.

SERVES 6 74 calories, 4.5g carbs, 5.8g fat, 0.8g sat fat, 1.2g protein

Turkish Chopped Salad (recipe on page 125)

Heritage Tomatoes with Basil and Balsamic Vinegar

HERITAGE TOMATOES WITH BASIL AND BALSAMIC VINEGAR

I am very specific about the kind of tomatoes I like to cook with as there is such a diversity of types and each can bring a distinct character to a dish. My preference is for slightly tart varieties – the Kumato or Green Zebra. The orange heritage (Persimmon) tomatoes tend to be less acidic, the orangey-yellow (Rainbow) ones are sweet, and the big fleshy red ones (beefsteak or Brandywine) are well-balanced all-rounders. Quality is also important, as bland, under-ripe, mealy tomatoes are no good for anything, that's for sure. And don't forget to use vinegar, be it balsamic, sherry, red wine or malt, as it really does help to highlight the flavour. Also look out for, and taste, the Italian Moscatel wine vinegar – it's a light vinegar, not too different to a sherry vinegar, with a slightly sweet, fruity taste.

2 large sweet heritage tomatoes – red, golden or orange
2 tablespoons thick, syrupy balsamic vinegar
2 tablespoons extra virgin olive oil
pinch of chilli flakes
15g basil, stalks removed
sea salt and freshly cracked black pepper

Slice the tomatoes, removing the hard core where necessary. Layer the tomatoes on a large serving platter and drizzle over the vinegar and oil and scatter over the chilli flakes. Season to taste with salt and pepper and leave to stand for 10 minutes.

Sprinkle over the basil leaves, tearing any large leaves into smaller pieces, and serve.

SERVES 4 68 calories, 3.7g carbs, 5.6g fat, 0.8g sat fat, 0.5g protein

You could also serve the sliced tomatoes with any of these three alternative toppings:

CAPERS AND PARSLEY

Soak 3 tablespoons salt-cured capers in hot water for 10 minutes, then drain and pat dry. In a frying pan, heat 4 tablespoons extra virgin olive oil. Add the capers and cook until they start to pop, then remove and set aside. Take the pan off the heat and stir in 2 tablespoons red wine vinegar. Pour the oil and vinegar over the sliced tomatoes and then scatter with the popped capers and 3 tablespoons chopped flat-leaf parsley. Finish with a grind of freshly cracked black pepper.

SERVES 4 115 calories, 2.6g carbs, 11g fat, 1.6g sat fat, 0.8g protein

ANCHOVY AND CRACKED GREEN OLIVES

Drain 4 anchovy fillets in oil and place in a frying pan with 3 tablespoons extra virgin olive oil. Cook, mashing gently with a wooden spoon, until the anchovies dissolve, then stir in 3 tablespoons red wine vinegar and 100g cracked, pitted green olives. Pour over the sliced tomatoes and season with freshly cracked black pepper.

SERVES 4 118 calories, 2.3g carbs, 11.3g fat, 1.6g sat fat, 1.4g protein

BREADCRUMB GREMOLATA

Heat 2 tablespoons extra virgin olive oil in a frying pan and cook 50g fresh breadcrumbs slowly for 5–8 minutes until golden and crisp, stirring every 2–3 minutes. Remove from the heat and set aside to cool. Season with sea salt, the finely grated zest of 1 lemon and 2 tablespoons finely chopped flat-leaf parsley, dill or chives. Drizzle the sliced tomatoes with 2 tablespoons extra virgin olive oil and a splash of malt vinegar, and scatter the crisp breadcrumb gremolata over the top.

SERVES 4 140 calories, 8.5g carbs, 11.3g fat, 1.6g sat fat, 1.5g protein

CHERRY TOMATOES WITH OREGANO AND BLACK OLIVES

The best time for cherry tomatoes is in the late summer when they are as sweet as can be. I also love the multi-coloured baby varieties, as each tomato provides a contrasting note of sharp and sweet. Serve with grilled meats, fish and poultry.

4 tablespoons extra virgin olive oil
1 tablespoon sesame seeds
100g salt-cured black olives, pitted
2 tablespoons sherry vinegar
500g cherry tomatoes on the vine, or multi-coloured baby
  tomatoes, cut in half
2 tablespoons oregano leaves
sea salt and freshly cracked black pepper

Heat the oil in a frying pan and cook the sesame seeds until toasted. Take the pan off the heat and stir in the olives and vinegar.

To a large bowl, add all the tomatoes, pour over the dressing and toss well. Stir in the oregano leaves, season to taste and leave to stand for 10 minutes – for all the flavours to come together. Serve.

SERVES 4 172 calories, 4.6g carbs, 16.1g fat, 2.4g sat fat, 2.2g protein

TOMATO AND DILL SALAD

This is a simple salad; I often serve it as a bruschetta, spooned over toasted crusty bread. Or serve as a topping for barbecued meat, poultry or fish.

3 Kumato or Green Zebra tomatoes, diced
2 tablespoons extra virgin olive oil
1 tablespoon malt vinegar
15g dill, chopped
15g flat-leaf parsley, chopped
100g feta, crumbled
sea salt and freshly cracked black pepper
toasted crusty bread, cut into fingers, to serve

Place the tomatoes in a bowl, drizzle with the oil and vinegar and season with salt and pepper. Set aside for 10 minutes.

Fold in the dill, parsley and feta and spoon onto fingers of toasted crusty bread. Leave to stand for another 5 minutes, for the juices to seep into the toast, and serve.

SERVES 4 124 calories, 2.4g carbs, 10.7g fat, 4.2g sat fat, 4.5g protein

Tomato with Dill Salad

Courgette and Parmesan Carpaccio (recipe on page 134)

COURGETTE AND PARMESAN CARPACCIO

In the summer, young courgettes are extremely tender and sweet and need very little preparation whatsoever. This is a perfect no-cook starter or side salad and goes deliciously with grilled meats and fish.

350g mixed courgettes in season – yellow, light green
   or stripy
juice of 1 lemon
5 tablespoons extra virgin olive oil
2 tablespoons salted capers, soaked and drained
3 tablespoons roughly chopped hazelnuts
50g Parmesan, grated on a microplane or finely grated
sea salt and freshly cracked black pepper

Using a mandolin, slice the courgettes very thinly and arrange on a large serving platter. Drizzle over the lemon juice and half the olive oil.

In a frying pan, heat the remaining oil and fry the capers until they pop. Remove with a slotted spoon and drain on kitchen paper. Add the hazelnuts to the oil and sauté until toasted, then drain on kitchen paper.

Season the courgettes with salt and pepper and scatter over the capers, hazelnuts and Parmesan. Allow to stand for another 5 minutes and then serve.

SERVES 4 242 calories, 2.4g carbs, 22.6g fat, 4.8g sat fat, 7.4g protein

ARTICHOKE SALAD

Artichokes are in my top ten foods. They were always served as part of our big family meals – each one was quartered and soaked in lemony water (the hairy choke discarded) with leaves still attached. They were then put on the table at the last minute with extra lemon and salt, and all you had to do was snap the leaves, bite the tips and discard the rest of the leaves. The crunchy heart of the vegetable was the very best and I always placed this on the side of my plate until the end of the meal, saving the best until last. Serve this salad warm or cold, or mix in with a bowl of homemade pasta (see pages 66–67).

3–4 young, medium-sized artichokes, stalks removed
juice of 2 lemons
3 tablespoons extra virgin olive oil
1 garlic clove, smashed
2 tablespoons finely grated Parmesan
sea salt and freshly cracked black pepper

To prepare the artichokes, remove all the leaves and discard. Using a spoon, scoop out the hairy chokes and discard. Rub the artichoke hearts all over with lemon juice and then soak in a bowl of lemon water.

Using a mandolin or vegetable peeler, thinly shave two of the hearts and pat dry with kitchen paper.

In a large frying pan, heat 2 tablespoons of the oil and add the garlic. Swirl the clove around in the oil to flavour it, then remove and discard. Add the shaved artichoke hearts to the pan and sauté for 3–5 minutes until they start to brown and caramelise.

Meanwhile, shave the remaining artichoke hearts and pat dry. Place in a shallow bowl, add the cooked artichoke and toss together. Season to taste with salt and pepper, drizzle with the remaining oil, top with the grated Parmesan, and serve.

SERVES 4 115 calories, 3.1g carbs, 9.9g fat, 2.2g sat fat, 4.8g protein

PUNTARELLE AND ANCHOVY SALAD

Puntarelle is a winter salad leaf that comes in a large bulbous head, the thickness of a Chinese cabbage. However, it tastes nothing like it as it belongs to the chicoria (endive) family and so has strong bitter-tasting leaves. To prepare, pick and wash the long stems and strip the leaves. Cut the stems into thin strips and soak in ice-cold water for an hour until they curl and become crisp, with some of the bitterness removed. I love the bitterness and therefore, when I am short of time, I often don't bother with the soaking or stripping of the leaves. Serve as a starter with crusty bread, or as a side with grilled chicken or fish.

1 head of puntarelle, leaves prepared as per intro

FOR THE DRESSING
3 salt-cured anchovies, filleted (see page 34)
3 tablespoons red wine vinegar
1 garlic clove, mashed with salt
4 tablespoons extra virgin olive oil, plus extra to serve
sea salt and freshly cracked black pepper

Pat dry the prepared puntarelle on kitchen paper and place in a large bowl.

In a separate bowl, for the dressing, use a fork to mash the anchovies into the vinegar. Add the garlic, followed by the oil and whisk together before seasoning to taste.

Toss the puntarelle with the dressing and leave to stand for 10 minutes for the flavours to develop. Serve with a little more extra virgin olive oil drizzled over the top.

SERVES 6 80 calories, 0.6g carbs, 7.7g fat, 1.1g sat fat, 1.6g protein

FENNEL AND BLOOD ORANGE SALAD

This is a classic Italian combination and makes the perfect starter.

10 salt-cured black olives, pitted
3 tablespoons extra virgin olive oil
2–4 young fennel bulbs, or 2 medium-sized bulbs, trimmed
juice of ½ orange
2 tablespoons red wine vinegar
2–3 blood oranges, depending on size
150g rocket, chopped
Parmesan, grated on a microplane or finely grated
  (optional)
sea salt and freshly cracked black pepper

Preheat the oven to 200°C/400°F/gas mark 6.

Place the olives in a small baking dish and toss to coat with 2 tablespoons of the oil. Roast for 15 minutes until plump.

Meanwhile, using a mandolin, thinly slice the fennel (about 3mm thick) and, if it falls apart, don't worry. Place in a bowl and toss with the orange juice, vinegar and remaining oil. Allow to stand for 10 minutes.

With a sharp knife, remove all the rind and pith from the blood oranges and then slice them into discs and arrange on a large serving plate.

Add the rocket and seasoning to the fennel and toss to mix. Spoon the salad over the orange slices and drizzle over any dressing left in the bowl. Top with the roasted black olives and, if you're feeling indulgent, a sprinkle of Parmesan to serve.

SERVES 4 118 calories, 5.4g carbs, 9.5g fat, 1.4g sat fat, 2.8g protein

WATERMELON, WATERCRESS AND SESAME SALAD

Purslane is a mild, sweet green salad leaf that grows wild almost everywhere. It has a slightly slippery texture and its sweet flavour is such a perfect contrast to peppery watercress that I love to pair them together. This salad makes a great starter and you can add crumbled feta or grated halloumi for even more flavour.

300g ripe watermelon flesh, chopped into 2–3cm pieces
2 tablespoons sherry vinegar
3 tablespoons extra virgin olive oil
100g purslane
100g watercress
15g flat-leaf parsley
15g mint sprigs
2 tablespoons sesame seeds, toasted
sea salt and freshly cracked black pepper

In a large bowl, place the watermelon and toss with the vinegar and oil. Season with salt and pepper and leave to stand for 10 minutes.

Separate the purslane, watercress and herbs into 5cm long sprigs. With a slotted spoon, transfer the watermelon onto a large serving platter, reserving the juices.

Add all the salad leaves and herbs to the bowl with the dressing and toss to mix. Spoon over the melon pieces and drizzle all over with the juices. Sprinkle with sesame seeds and serve.

SERVES 4 147 calories, 5.9g carbs, 12.4g fat, 2g sat fat, 3.2g protein

WATERMELON AND FETA SALAD

In recent years, a watermelon salad has become a fashionable summer dish. However, when I was growing up, chilled watermelon was always a refreshing snack or part of a picnic lunch on the beach, eaten with hunks of halloumi, black salty olives and crusty bread. Therefore, I think the watermelon salad is more of an Australian invention than a Mediterranean one, but as it is so good, and contains all the flavours of the Mediterranean, I felt I had to include it here.

675g watermelon, cut into wedges
4 tablespoons extra virgin olive oil
25g mint leaves, torn
150g feta cheese, broken into chunks
edible herb flowers, such as peppery radish or rocket
lemon juice or balsamic vinegar, to serve
sea salt and freshly cracked black pepper

Using a sharp knife, cut away the green skin and rind from the watermelon up to where the white flesh starts to turn pink. Slice the flesh into 1.5cm thick triangles and layer on a large serving platter. Drizzle with olive oil, season with salt and pepper and sprinkle over the mint, feta and herb flowers. Finish with a fresh squeeze of lemon juice or a splash of balsamic vinegar.

SERVES 4 234 calories, 9.8g carbs, 19g fat, 6.8g sat fat, 6.7g protein

Watermelon and Feta Salad

Autumn-Winter Salad

AUTUMN-WINTER SALAD

Autumn brings us salad leaves that have quite a bitter or peppery taste, and this flavour is strong enough to brilliantlly balance out rich wintry stews, grilled steaks and meatballs. They often have a crisp texture too and are excellent served with a joint of roasted meat.

300g mixed leaves, such as romaine, radicchio, treviso, dandelion, rocket, baby kale and mustard leaves
50g mixed herbs, such as flat-leaf parsley, mint, oregano or marjoram and rocket flowers
sea salt and freshly cracked black pepper

FOR THE DRESSING
2 garlic cloves, crushed with salt or grated on a microplane
1 shallot, finely chopped
3 tablespoons red wine or sherry vinegar
4 tablespoons extra virgin olive oil

Tear or chop the salad leaves into 5–7cm pieces and place in a large bowl. Mix together all the dressing ingredients in a separate bowl and toss into the salad leaves. Fold in the herbs and rocket flowers, if available, and season to taste. Serve.

SERVES 4 121 calories, 2.1g carbs, 11.3g fat, 1.6g sat fat, 2.3g protein

SPRING-SUMMER SALAD

This salad makes the most of the season's first young crop of vegetables – fresh, tender broad beans, peas and asparagus. Serve as a side with grilled fish or with a creamy ball of burrata, or even stir it into a bowl of homemade pasta.

1 shallot, thinly sliced
3 tablespoons red wine or sherry vinegar
4 tablespoons extra virgin olive oil
750g broad beans, podded and skins removed if necessary
750g fresh peas, podded
225g asparagus, trimmed
100g mixed pea or broad bean tendrils, watercress, rocket, radish leaves or purslane
100g mixed salad flowers, such as peppery nasturtiums, courgette flowers, borage flowers, marigolds
200g Little Gem lettuce, leaves separated
25g mint
15g flat-leaf parsley
50g chopped pistachios
sea salt and freshly cracked black pepper

First make the dressing. Place the shallot in a small bowl and stir in the vinegar with a little salt and pepper. Allow to stand for 10 minutes, and then stir in the oil.

Place the broad beans and peas in a large bowl and pour over all the dressing and toss. Allow to stand for 10 minutes.

Using a vegetable peeler or mandolin, shave the asparagus into long strips, then add to the large bowl with the mixed leaves, flowers, lettuce, herbs and nuts and toss to mix. Taste and adjust the seasoning if necessary. Serve.

SERVES 4 340 calories, 20.5g carbs, 21.1g fat, 3.3g sat fat, 17.6g protein

Left: vegetable selection that includes broad
bean flowers and tendrils, asparagus, artichokes,
treviso lettuce, baby broccoli rapini, fairy
aubergines and rosemary; top centre: breakfast
radishes; bottom centre: capers preserved in salt;
top right: romaine or cos lettuce; bottom right:
mustard leaf

BARBECUED AND ROASTED VEGETABLES

I love to roast vegetables in a really hot oven or to barbecue them over hot charcoal – it's my favourite way to cook them as it provides good, even charring and caramelising and creates a layered sweet and savoury flavour. For greens especially, you can find the volume decreases to almost half the amount you started with, but the flavour makes it worth it.

When barbecuing, ensure you place a cake or cooling rack over the existing grill rack, as you need the narrower grates in order not to lose the vegetables through the gaps – it makes turning so much easier. Ensure the vegetables are rubbed well with extra virgin olive oil and flavourings, and use long tongs so you can pick up the vegetables easily. They don't need to cook for long, so don't walk away from the grill. See page 84 on how to preheat the charcoal grill.

With all the roasted vegetable recipes that follow, the flavourings and vegetables are all interchangeable.

BARBECUED FLAT BEANS

These flat beans can be young, tender runner beans or Romano beans (a tender flat bean in a pod) – excellent served with grilled or roasted meats, poultry and fish.

750g flat beans, topped and tailed
6 tablespoons extra virgin olive oil
50g Parmesan, grated on a microplane
2 tablespoons red wine vinegar
sea salt and freshly cracked black pepper

Preheat a charcoal grill and place a cooling rack over the top. Brush with oil.

If the beans are really long, cut them down to about 7cm long. Place the beans in a bowl and drizzle with half the oil and season with salt and pepper. Toss to coat thoroughly.

Line the beans on top of the grill rack and cook the beans for 3 minutes until they are just charring in places. Turn the beans over and cook again until they are just charring; they should still be green in places. About 8 minutes cooking time in total is all that is needed.

Transfer to a serving plate and scatter with the Parmesan. Mix together the vinegar with the remaining oil and drizzle over the beans. Serve.

SERVES 4 243 calories, 6.2g carbs, 21g fat, 5g sat fat, 7.6g protein

Barbecued Flat Beans

Barbecued Broccoli Rapini

BARBECUED BROCCOLI RAPINI

Broccoli rapini is a long-stemmed leafy broccoli with a bitter-peppery taste. It is widely used all over Italy and the USA and now, I'm happy to say, is becoming more popular in the UK, where it's known as wild broccoli. (You could use tenderstem or sprouting broccoli as an alternative, but it won't be so leafy.) It's served on pizza, with pasta and sausage, or by itself as a side with roasted meats and fish.

You can also roast the broccoli rapini. Cook on two large baking trays, in a preheated hot oven at 220°C/425°F/gas mark 7 for 20 minutes.

3 tablespoons extra virgin olive oil, plus extra to serve
750g broccoli rapini, washed and trimmed
3 garlic cloves, mashed with salt
2 teaspoons Calabrian chilli flakes
sea salt and freshly cracked black pepper
lemon juice, to serve (optional)

Preheat the charcoal grill and place a cooling rack over the grill rack. Once the flames die down, brush with oil.

Trim the broccoli stems to 7cm lengths, or keep longer if you want. Place on a baking tray, drizzle over the olive oil and use your hands to rub in the garlic and chilli flakes. Season with black pepper and a little more salt – but bear in mind that you have already used some with the garlic that was mashed with salt!

Arrange the broccoli on the grill and cook for 10 minutes, turning every 3 minutes and once it begins to char. The broccoli should be charred in places but bright green in others, and tender with a little chewiness. Pile onto a serving plate and drizzle with a little more extra virgin olive oil and lemon juice (if using) to serve.

SERVES 4 142 calories, 6.6g carbs, 9.5g fat, 1.5g sat fat, 8.5g protein

BARBECUED MIXED VEGETABLES

This Italian barbecued vegetable platter, steeped in extra virgin olive oil, is now a very common salad dish served as part of an antipasti selection in Italian restaurants. The correct way to prepare them is to barbecue/grill them plain at first, just with oil, and then they should sit in a single layer, marinating in extra virgin olive oil, garlic and herbs.

1 red pepper, cored, deseeded and quartered
1 yellow pepper, cored, deseeded and quartered
2 yellow courgettes, topped, tailed and each cut into
   3 long slices
2 green courgettes, topped, tailed and each cut into
   3 long slices
1 medium aubergine, sliced into 1cm-thick rounds
150ml extra virgin olive oil
2 dried chillies
3 garlic cloves, bashed to split the skins
1 teaspoon lightly crushed black peppercorns
1 teaspoon lightly crushed pink peppercorns
sea salt
toasted crusty bread, to serve

Preheat a charcoal grill, place a cooling rack with narrow grates over the grill rack and brush with oil.

Brush the vegetables on all sides with some of the oil and arrange over the hot grill in a single layer. Cook for 4–5 minutes on each side, brushing with more oil and seasoning with salt, until nicely charred and caramelised.

Transfer the vegetables to a large, shallow serving platter and arrange them in a single layer.

Heat the remaining oil in a small saucepan with the dried chillies, garlic and black and pink peppercorns. Once the oil is just hot, pour over the vegetables and set aside to cool to room temperature. Serve with crusty toasted bread.

SERVES 6 268 calories, 6.3g carbs, 25.8g fat, 3.7g sat fat, 3.1g protein

Picture on the left; dried oregano, fresh sage, extra virgin olive oil, clementines, red wine, butternut squash, and honeynut squash; bottom centre: fennel; bottom right: Roasted Squash (see page 148)

ROASTED SQUASH WITH CHILLI FLAKES

I recommend you use butternut, kabocha, acorn, crown prince or turban squash for this recipe. With its chestnut flavour and potato-like texture, kabocha is my favourite, but of course butternut squash is a great all-rounder too. As I am quite a lazy cook, I often can't be bothered to peel the squash, so I wash the outside well, halve it down the middle and scoop out the seeds, and then I roast the squash in large pieces still in its skin. When I serve it like this, friends who don't like the skin just leave it on the side, so there's no harm done. All roasted squash are a good side to roasts or as an addition to grain dishes or pilafs (see page 54 for grain bowls).

750g squash of your choice, cut into large chunks
3 tablespoons extra virgin olive oil
1–2 teaspoons chilli flakes
sea salt and freshly cracked black pepper

Preheat the oven to 220°C/425°F/gas mark 7. Arrange the squash on 1–2 shallow baking trays, depending on the size of your oven, and drizzle with the oil. Use your hands to rub the oil in with the chilli flakes and seasoning until each piece is well coated.

Roast the squash for 25–30 minutes, turning after 20 minutes (and switch round the trays if you're using two). The squash is perfect when evenly caramelised and with some charring in places. A fork inserted into the squash should go through easily. Serve straightaway.

SERVES 4 142 calories, 15.6g carbs, 8.6g fat, 1.2g sat fat, 2.2g protein

CHARRED MIXED GREENS WITH FENNEL AND LEMONS

Dandelion, spinach, mustard and even rocket leaves all roast really well. They do cook right down but the flavour is so intense, it's delicious and satisfying. Combined with sliced fennel and lemon, these vegetables are perfect served with roasted or grilled fish or chicken.

1kg mixed greens, washed and dried
2 small fennel bulbs, trimmed and cut into 3mm-thick slices
2 small lemons, trimmed and cut into 3mm-thick slices
3 tablespoons extra virgin olive oil
sea salt and freshly cracked black pepper

Preheat the oven to 220°C/425°F/gas mark 7. Cut the greens into 7cm-lengths but no shorter as they really will shrink. It looks like a huge mound, but they will reduce. Divide the greens between two shallow baking trays and add the fennel and lemon slices. Drizzle over the oil and seasoning and use your hands to rub in well to coat.

Roast the vegetables for 30 minutes, using tongs to toss after 15 minutes. There will be lots of liquid released and yet, by the end of the cooking time, this will have evaporated and the fennel should be tender, with a slight chewiness and a little charred in places. Serve straightaway.

SERVES 4 125 calories, 2.2g carbs, 9.9g fat, 1.4 sat fat, 7.2g protein

ROASTED CAULIFLOWER STEAKS

There is now a big influx of heritage cauliflowers hitting the vegetable stands, so look out for purple, orange, green and cone-shaped Romanesco varieties. Each type varies in sweetness and flavour and also provides different nutrients.

3 tablespoons pine nuts
3 tablespoons extra virgin olive oil
1–2 medium tight heads of cauliflower, trimmed
4 garlic cloves, smashed with salt flakes
sea salt and freshly cracked black pepper

FOR THE DRESSING
1 x 40g can anchovies in olive oil, drained
4 tablespoons red wine vinegar
6 tablespoons extra virgin olive oil
2 tablespoons chopped flat-leaf parsley
2 tablespoons salted capers, soaked and drained

Preheat the oven to 220°C/425°F/gas mark 7. Spread the pine nuts out over a baking tray and roast for 5 minutes, keeping a close eye as the oven temperature is high. Set aside.

Meanwhile, holding the cauliflower upright, use a sharp knife to slice about 1–2cm off each side and then cut the rest into four thick slices or 'steaks'. Be careful to keep all the florets attached to the stem.

Place the cauliflower steaks on 1–2 baking trays, drizzle over the oil, season and then rub all over with the smashed garlic. Cover each tray with a sheet of parchment paper, then place another baking tray on top, and weigh down with a cast-iron frying pan. Place in the oven and roast for 30 minutes, turning the steaks after 20 minutes, until evenly caramelised.

Meanwhile, make the dressing. Place the anchovies in a small bowl and mash with a fork. Add the vinegar to the anchovies and then whisk in the olive oil. Add the parsley, capers and toasted pine nuts and adjust the seasoning if necessary. Serve the cauliflower steaks with the dressing.

SERVES 4 336 calories, 6.8g carbs, 31.2g fat, 4.1g sat fat, 6.7g protein

BARBECUED SPRING ONIONS

Spring onions are some of my favourite things to grill on the barbecue as they cook so quickly, you don't have to worry about losing them between the grates and they go so well with all kinds of foods – roasted or grilled fish, shellfish, chicken or lamb. Keep an eye out for the purple-tipped spring onions when they're in season in the summer.

20 spring onions, trimmed with the roots left intact
3 tablespoons extra virgin olive oil
1 tablespoon Colatura di Alici (anchovy sauce)
2 tablespoons toasted sesame seeds
sea salt and freshly cracked black pepper

Preheat the charcoal grill. Place a cooling rack over the grill rack and brush with oil.

Use your hands to rub the spring onions with half the oil, season with salt and pepper and then place on the hot grill rack. Turn after 3 minutes when the onions should have started to char. Keep an eye on them as they cook quickly! Cook for another 3 minutes and then transfer to a serving plate.

In a small bowl, mix the remaining oil with the anchovy sauce. Pour over the spring onions, sprinkle over the sesame seeds and serve straightaway.

SERVES 4 123 calories, 1.7g carbs, 12g fat, 1.9g sat fat, 2.3g protein

Whole Roasted Onions (recipe on page 152)

WHOLE ROASTED ONIONS

Walking through the markets in Sicily, especially those of Catania, the stalls are always piled high with trays of roasted onions, aubergines and courgettes. I always like the look of the large onions and ask, 'How does one eat these?' 'Oh, take home and make into a sandwich.' And so I can taste the delicious crusty bread and melting triple-milk cheese, or perhaps a good walnut pesto, or roasted meat or fish.

3 medium red onions
3 medium yellow onions
2 tablespoons extra virgin olive oil
crusty bread, to serve

FOR THE WALNUT PESTO
100g walnuts, toasted
2 garlic cloves, smashed with salt (optional)
100g rocket or flat-leaf parsley, or a mixture,
    roughly chopped
juice of ½ lemon
pinch of Calabrian chilli flakes
100ml extra virgin olive oil
50g finely grated Parmesan or pecorino (optional)
sea salt and freshly cracked black pepper

Preheat the oven to 200°C/400°F/gas mark 6. Wash the onions, but leave their skins on with the root and everything and use your hands to rub them all over with oil. Pack them snugly in a shallow baking tray and roast for 45 minutes, until charred in places and almost bursting – they should be tender inside.

Meanwhile, make the pesto. Place the walnuts in a food-processor and pulse twice to chop slightly. Add the garlic (if using), and rocket or parsley and whizz once more. Add the lemon juice and a sprinkling of chilli flakes and, with the processor running, drizzle in the oil to form a semi-thick pesto. Spoon the pesto into a bowl, add the cheese, (if using), and season. Serve with the onions and some crusty bread.

SERVES 6 128 calories, 12g carbs, 3.8g fat, 0.8g sat fat, 2.2g protein
WALNUT PESTO 281 calories, 0.9g carbs, 29.3g fat, 3.7g sat fat, 3.5g protein

SESAME-ROASTED SWISS CHARD

You can also swap the Swiss chard for rainbow Swiss chard or beetroot leaves.

675g Swiss chard
4 tablespoons extra virgin olive oil
3 tablespoons balsamic vinegar
3 tablespoons sesame seeds
sea salt and freshly cracked black pepper

Preheat the oven to 220°C/425°F/gas mark 7. Wash the chard well to remove all the grit. Drain and pat dry with kitchen paper.

Chop the chard into 7cm pieces and spread out over two shallow baking trays. Drizzle over the oil and vinegar and sprinkle over the sesame seeds and seasoning. Use your hands to rub all the ingredients into the leaves and stems.

Roast in the oven for 25 minutes, tossing with tongs and turning the trays around twice. Check that the leaves have crisped, the stems have become tender and the seeds are toasted. Transfer to a serving plate and serve.

SERVES 4 195 calories, 7g carbs, 16.6g fat, 2.5g sat fat, 4.8g protein

Sesame-roasted Swiss Chard

MAKE IT SLOW/TAKE IT SLOW

Slow-cooked meats and pulses (dried beans, peas and lentils) are highly prized in Mediterranean cooking, as they prove just how much you can achieve with a few very simple (and often cheap) ingredients and a little patience. As a kid, being raised in London, I remember going to the butcher's with my grandmother. She did not speak a word of English and yet somehow she managed to buy pork shoulder blade bone and lamb and pork shanks, which the butcher chopped for her into a few pieces. There was only a tiny amount of meat on the bone and yet for my grandmother, that was perfect. From that bone she made broths and stocks, and bases for her soups, braises and pasta dishes that were very comforting to all us young cousins growing up together. The bone, which so many cooks discard as kitchen waste, contributed an intensity of flavour that very few ingredients or flavourings can match. In the same way, my mother would always serve bucatini in some kind of chicken or meat-bone broth. Until I was about 18, I had no idea that pasta was cooked mainly just in water with a sauce on top! And this is the principle behind many classic Mediterranean soups, stews and braises. All these dishes are well worth the wait.

BRAISED MIXED GREEN LEAVES

I like to cook greens in the oven (see page 148 for charred Mixed Greens). However, my other preferred method, and especially for beetroot tops, is in a large sauté pan over a very low heat. This also works for all types of Swiss chard, Tuscan kale, dandelion (in fact, all bitter leaves), spinach (although not baby or pousse) and agretti (although the latter, I like to cook by itself rather than in a mix). You can serve these greens warm or cold, folded into grains of all kinds or as a side to chicken, meat or fish, cooked whichever way you choose.

1kg greens of your choice (see above), single or mixed
4 tablespoons extra virgin olive oil
2 garlic cloves, bashed
2 shallots, roughly chopped
juice of 1 lemon
sea salt and freshly cracked black pepper

Fill the sink with cold water and wash the greens well as you will find they are quite muddy and gritty. Strip the stems from the leaves and separate the two. Trim the stems and pat dry on kitchen paper and dry the leaves too, or spin-dry in a salad spinner. Roughly cut both the leaves and stems into 3cm-wide strips.

Heat half the oil in a large sauté pan with a lid and, once sizzling, add the garlic and fry until it starts to colour, then remove and discard the garlic. Add the shallots and stems to the flavoured oil and cook for 5–8 minutes, until just beginning to turn golden. Add the leaves and toss together all the ingredients with tongs as this makes the lifting and turning action much easier. Once coated with oil, season well with salt and pepper.

Cover the pan and cook over a low heat for 30 minutes, stirring once more, halfway through and seasoning to taste. Serve with a squeeze of lemon juice and a drizzle of the remaining oil.

SERVES 4 187 calories, 8.7g carbs, 13.6g fat, 1.8g sat fat, 8g protein

SLOW-COOKED BEETROOT WITH FETA

In spring and early autumn, when beetroot are young and small, my laziness takes over and I don't peel the bulbs. I simply wash them well, ensuring all the grit is scrubbed away, and then I slice them down the middle. When cooked, the skin comes off the vegetable very easily and so you can choose to eat the skin or leave it on the side of the plate. This dish makes a flavoursome starter, or mixed into a grain, a satisfying vegetarian main course.

750g small beetroot, cleaned and cut in half
2 tablespoons coriander seeds, lightly crushed
a pinch of Calabrian chilli flakes
4 tablespoons extra virgin olive oil, plus extra to finish
3 tablespoons sherry or malt vinegar
150g sliced feta
sea salt and freshly cracked black pepper

Preheat the oven to 180°C/350°F/gas mark 4. Take a large piece of parchment paper, scrunch it up, hold it under cold running water and then shake off the excess drips. Open out the paper and use it to line a heavy sauté pan with a lid.

Place the prepared beetroot in the paper. Sprinkle over the coriander seeds and chilli flakes, drizzle with oil and vinegar and season. (I don't mix any further as I don't want to discolour everything, especially my hands!) Take another large piece of wet parchment and place over the top. Cover with the heavy lid, allowing the paper to hang down over the side. Place the pan in the oven and braise the beetroot for 2 hours until tender.

Remove the lid and top piece of parchment. Scatter the feta over the beetroot, drizzle with a little more oil and serve either warm or cold.

SERVES 4 263 calories, 14.9g carbs, 19.2g fat, 6.7g sat fat, 9.5g protein

Slow-cooked Beetroot with Feta

Poached Artichokes with Capers

POACHED ARTICHOKES WITH CAPERS

Poached artichokes taste delicious and they're very simple to prepare – perfect for a starter or healthy midday snack. I like to serve them warm or at room temperature with a dressing that doubles up as a dip – caper and parsley, mustard vinaigrette, or anchovy and shallot, in fact, almost all the dressings and sauces I use to serve with fish (see pages 96–99).

15g mixed dried mushrooms
8 small artichokes or 4 large, washed
3 salt-cured anchovies, filleted (see page 34) and chopped
4 tablespoons moscatel or sherry vinegar
4 tablespoons chopped flat-leaf parsley
6 tablespoons extra virgin olive oil
sea salt and freshly cracked black pepper

Place the mushrooms in a large saucepan, fill the pan with water and bring to the boil (to make a quick and simple stock). Add the artichokes and simmer for 20 minutes if small and 40 minutes if large. There are two ways to test for doneness; pull on an inner leaf and, if it comes away easily, the artichoke should be ready. Alternatively, insert a fork into the base of the artichoke and, if it goes through easily, it's done. Lift out with a slotted spoon and set aside until cool enough to handle.

Meanwhile, make the dressing by mixing together the anchovies, vinegar, parsley and 4 tablespoons of the extra virgin olive oil. Taste, and season with a little salt and pepper.

Place the artichokes on a large platter or individual plates and gently ease open the leaves so you can scoop out the central hairy choke with a spoon. Drizzle about a tablespoon of the dressing into the middle of each artichoke and serve the remainder on the side. Drizzle the remaining olive oil, season with salt and pepper and serve.

SERVES 4 191 calories, 8.8 carbs, 16.1g fat, 2.4g sat fat, 4.2g protein

SPRING BRAISED CHICKEN WITH ARTICHOKES, PEAS AND BROAD BEANS

You can cook the chicken and artichokes up to 24 hours in advance, then simply add the peas and broad beans when reheating to serve.

4 chicken leg and thigh quarters
4 tablespoons extra virgin olive oil
3 garlic cloves, bashed to split the skins
50g pancetta or guanciale, chopped
4 artichoke hearts, or 8 small ones (prepare as per Artichoke Salad on page 134)
350ml chicken stock
225g fresh podded peas
225g fresh podded broad beans
salt and freshly cracked black pepper
extra virgin olive oil and chopped flat-leaf parsley and mint, to serve

Preheat the oven to 180°C/350°F/gas mark 4. Season the chicken with salt and pepper. Heat the oil in a large sauté pan and add the garlic cloves. Cook the garlic for 3 minutes to flavour the oil. Remove the garlic and discard.

Add the chicken to the pan and sear all over, about 10–15 minutes. Remove and drain. Remove all but 2 tablespoons of the fat from the pan. Add the pancetta or guanciale to the pan and cook for 5 minutes. Return the chicken to the pan with the artichokes. Add the chicken stock and bring to the boil. Cover with wet parchment paper (see page 156), then the lid. Transfer to the oven and cook for 45 minutes until the chicken and artichokes are tender.

Stir the peas and broad beans into the pan. Cook for another 10 minutes. Serve drizzled with extra virgin olive oil, and sprinkle with chopped flat-leaf parsley and mint.

SERVES 4 517 kcal, 13.7g carbs, 35.3g fat, 8.4g sat fat, 39.4g protein

STUFFED ARTICHOKES WITH MORELS
AND PANCETTA

There are two seasons for artichokes – the spring is for the young tender artichokes and the autumn for the larger variety. This dish is one for the autumn and, although the preparation can be a little time-consuming at first, it's well worth the effort. However, I do recommend that you wear rubber gloves for the task as they do discolour your hands. Also, don't waste the stalks. Simply peel back the stringy outer skin, dress the tender stems with lemon, sprinkle with salt and enjoy while you're making the dish.

15g dried morel mushrooms

4 large artichokes

1 lemon, squeezed and mixed with cold water in a bowl to make lemon water

4 tablespoons extra virgin olive oil, plus extra to finish

100g pancetta or guanciale, chopped

4 small shallots, finely chopped

75ml Marsala wine

2 large leeks, cleaned and cut into 5cm pieces

3 celery sticks, cut into 5cm pieces

3 medium carrots, peeled and cut into 5cm pieces

100g Umbrian (small green) dried lentils, washed and drained

freshly cracked black pepper

Place the dried mushrooms in a large bowl and cover with 500ml boiling water. Leave to stand for 15 minutes and then drain through a fine sieve lined with kitchen paper. Reserve the liquid; pat dry, then finely chop the mushrooms and set aside.

To prepare the artichokes, cut off the large stem if there is one and, depending on how tender or young the artichokes are, slice the leaves about a third of the way down to remove any toughness. Peel off and discard the outer leaves. With a teaspoon, dig down firmly into the centre and scoop out the inner leaves and hairy choke. Place the artichokes

immediately in a bowl of lemon water, as otherwise they will discolour quickly, and set aside until ready to cook.

Heat the oil in a large, deep pan with a lid, add the pancetta or guanciale and cook for 10 minutes until just beginning to brown. Remove with a slotted spoon and place in a bowl. Sauté the shallots in the oil until just beginning to brown and then add the chopped mushrooms and cook for 5 minutes. Again, remove with a slotted spoon and transfer to the bowl with the pancetta. Stir together well, and season with pepper. Use this mixture to stuff into the middle of each (drained) artichoke and then set aside.

Add the Marsala wine to the pan juices and heat to deglaze the pan. Scrape the bits in the pan, stirring for 2 minutes. Add the leeks, celery, carrots and lentils. Add the reserved mushroom liquid and bring to the boil. Carefully fit the artichokes into the pan, standing them upright and packing them in snugly. Wet a piece of parchment paper with water and place over the top of the artichokes. Cover with a tight-fitting lid and simmer for 35–45 minutes. To test if an artichoke is ready, pierce the base of the artichoke with a sharp knife, if it pierces easily, with no resistance, the artichoke is tender.

Serve warm with the lentils, vegetables and cooking broth, and finish with a drizzle of extra virgin olive oil.

SERVES 4 325 calories, 26.9g carbs, 16.7g fat, 3.5g sat fat, 17.2g protein

ALL ABOUT PULSES: DRIED BEANS, PEAS AND LENTILS

The Mediterranean diet embraces a wide variety of pulses, from dried fava and borlotti (or cranberry) beans through to chickpeas and lentils. Sometimes they take pride of place in their own dishes, offering a great source of protein, as well as soluble fibre and many other minerals. It is common for them to be served with grilled and roasted meats, and canned or salt-cured fish.

'FRESH' PULSES

The growth of farmers' markets means that, at certain times of the year, we can have access to incredible fresh pulses, picked in their pods and ready to be podded at home. Of course, there is no need to pre-soak these beans and they will easily cook within an hour or less. Look out for them in early spring or towards the end of summer, but bear in mind that you only cook the beans and not the pods and so, if you buy 1.5kg in their pods, you will only be left with about a third of that amount in beans or peas.

DRIED FAVA BEANS

These are dried green broad beans. They are sold in three different forms. The first is dried with the skin on and these do need to be soaked and the tough outer skin removed before cooking. I find this a little too time-consuming and don't generally buy these. The second type is whole-dried without the skin and these beans need to be pre-soaked and will take about 2½ hours to cook. The third and final type, and the one I recommend and use all the time, are cracked fava beans. There is no pre-soaking required. You can find them in local Greek, Turkish or Lebanese shops and all you have to do is wash them and cook for about 45 minutes. See page 167 for Fava Bean Stew or page 29 for Fava Bean Dip.

DRIED WHITE BEANS

There are many different varieties of white beans. Haricot beans are small and white, cannellini beans are slightly longer and thinner, and butter beans are larger and also known as Gigantes or Greek white jumbo beans. Correctly or wrong,

I actually include borlotti or cranberry beans in this section. I treat them exactly the same as white beans. All need to be pre-soaked for 24 hours and then drained and washed before using. Depending on size, they will take 2–2½ hours to cook.

DRIED BLACK-EYED PEAS

In the Mediterranean, the black-eyed pea is cooked with Swiss chard to make a delicious soupy stew, or Louvi, as we call it in Cyprus (see page 167). In the US, it's often cooked with smoked pork and collard greens (kale or spring greens), which results in very different flavours. Both are delicious. Soak dried black-eyed peas for 24 hours before cooking, or look out for fresh peas, which are slightly green where the white is when dried.

CHICKPEAS

Chickpeas are essential as, of course, they form the base to hummus and, as far as I'm concerned, you need boiled fresh chickpeas to make the very best. Some people like to add bicarbonate of soda to the chickpeas while soaking as they believe this makes the final texture lighter. However, in our family, we found this left us with a rather bloated feeling and so we leave it out. My mum actually takes the skins off all the chickpeas after soaking, but it's so labour intensive that I skip this stage and don't find it makes a huge difference. My preferred variety to cook with is the small chickpea from Umbria and you need to pre-soak them for 24 hours.

LENTILS

Lentils are nutritional powerhouses, providing a great source of protein as well as many minerals. A wide range is available from various countries around the world. In Mediterranean cooking, the small, delicate Puy lentil from France or the small green Umbrian lentil is popular and often used in pilafs and soups. The Greeks prefer a larger type and use it to make the classic, deliciously rustic soup or stew 'Fakes'. You do need to wash the lentils, but no pre-soaking is required.

WOOD FIRE-COOKED PULSES

If you have access to a wood-fired oven, how lucky you are! For years, I have been searching out bean dishes cooked in a wood-fired oven, in restaurants, and always think the taste is second to none. Often, the beans are placed in the ovens to cook while they cool down overnight and so they're infused with an incredible wood-smoked flavour. They're then served with braised or roasted meats or stirred into sauces, such as 'pasta e fagioli'. Of course, a little effort is required, but you won't regret it.

4 tablespoons extra virgin olive oil
1 onion, quartered
3 garlic cloves, bashed to split the skins
3–4 fresh thyme or rosemary sprigs
500g dried beans or peas of your choice, soaked overnight and drained

Using a charcoal grill with a lid, pre-light a chimney-load of charcoal (see page 84). When hot, move the charcoal over to one side and add some cedar or hickory wood chips near the charcoal. Set the grill rack on top and close the lid over the grill. You start high, then just leave; you do not need to keep adding more charcoal over the cooking process.

Meanwhile, place a large braising pot over a high heat on the hob and add the oil, onion, garlic and herbs. Once the onions are sizzling and transparent, add the beans of your choice. Top up with plenty of water, at least 15cm above the beans, and bring to the boil, skimming the surface of any white foam that forms.

Remove the pot from the heat, cover with a lid and transfer to the barbecue. Place on the cooler side of the grill, not directly over the charcoal and cook for 3–4 hours. Stir once or twice.

Serve as per the Chorizo and Escarole for boiled beans and chickpeas (see pages 166), or stir into pasta dishes, or serve with grilled meats or fish.

SERVES 4 101 calories, 14.7g carbs, 2.8g fat, 0.4g sat fat, 5.2g protein

BRAISED WHITE BEANS WITH LAMB

If you prefer, you can swap the chops for diced pieces of lamb shoulder. Serve with a bitter green salad or Roasted Broccoli Rapini (see page 92).

1kg lamb shoulder or leg chops, each about 2.5cm thick
4 tablespoons extra virgin olive oil, plus extra to serve
1 onion, roughly chopped
500g dried white beans, soaked overnight and drained
3 garlic cloves, bashed and peeled
3 rosemary sprigs, plus extra to serve
1 lemon, sliced, plus extra to serve
sea salt and fresh cracked black pepper

Preheat the oven to 180°C/350°F/gas mark 4. Season the lamb with salt and pepper. Place a large pan with a lid on the hob, heat some of the oil and, working in batches, sear the lamb pieces for 5–8 minutes until evenly browned. Remove with a slotted spoon and drain on kitchen paper while searing the remaining lamb.

Remove all but 2 tablespoons of fat from the pan and cook the onion in the pan juices until just beginning to brown. Add the beans and cover with plenty of water, at least 10cm above the beans. Bring to the boil, skimming the surface of any froth. Add the meat to the pan, with the garlic, rosemary and lemon.

Scrunch up a large piece of parchment paper, soak it in water and then open it out. Place it in the pan, directly over the liquid and then cover with a tight-fitting lid. Transfer the pan to the oven and braise for 2½ hours. Halfway through, give the beans a stir and season with salt and pepper, then re-cover with parchment paper and the lid and continue to braise until the lamb and beans are very tender and the juices have thickened slightly. Serve with extra lemon, rosemary and olive oil.

SERVES 8 388 calories, 35.2g carbs, 18.1g fat, 6.4g sat fat, 23.4g protein

Far left: 'fresh' podded white haricot beans; left: Braised White Beans with Lamb (see page 163); above: cracked fava beans; top right: Umbrian chickpeas; bottom right: 'fresh' borlotti/cranberry beans; below: rosemary

WHITE BEANS WITH LEMON AND ONION

Serve the beans in their own right, supplemented with a can of tuna or mackerel, dressed with olive oil and parsley. Alternatively, serve as a side for grilled meats – the way the Tuscans like to do with Florentine steak.

500g dried white beans, soaked overnight and then drained
1 lemon, sliced
1 onion, quartered
2–3 sprigs of flat-leaf parsley or rosemary (optional)
a drizzle of extra virgin olive oil
sea salt and freshly cracked black pepper

Place the beans in a large pan with a lid and cover with plenty of cold water, at least 15cm above the beans. Bring the water to the boil, skimming the surface of any white foam. Once it comes to the boil, reduce the heat to a simmer – allow the liquid to have some movement.

Add the lemon slices, onion and herbs (if using) and cook, partially covered, for 1½–2 hours. Season halfway through with salt and pepper and stir in a drizzle of olive oil. The beans are ready when they are tender but not mushy. Choose any one of the following options:

Version 1: Drain the beans and transfer to a large serving platter or bowl. Adjust the seasoning to taste, drizzle with more extra virgin olive oil and sprinkle with chopped flat-leaf parsley.

Version 2: Drain the beans and fold in char-grilled courgettes and fennel. Dress with extra virgin olive oil, chopped parsley and lemon juice, to taste.

Version 3: 1 hour into the cooking time, add 500g peeled and quartered potatoes and 500g chopped courgettes (cut into 7.5cm pieces), and continue to cook the beans until all the ingredients are tender. Serve the beans and vegetables in bowls with a ladle of the broth and a drizzle of extra virgin olive oil and lemon juice.

SERVES 6 253 calories, 43.7g carbs, 1.9g fat, 0.3g sat fat, 18.2g protein

BEANS WITH CHORIZO AND ESCAROLE

This recipe can be made with white beans, chickpeas or borlotti beans. The dried beans are cooked with a spicy sausage and tomatoes, then towards the end, a bitter leaf like escarole or dandelion is added. Serve as a soup or stew.

500g dried beans, soaked overnight and drained
3 tablespoons extra virgin olive oil
1 large onion, roughly chopped
150g dried chorizo, skin removed and sliced into
  3mm-thick slices
400g can plum tomatoes
1 head of escarole, dandelion leaves or other bitter leaves,
  about 300g
sea salt and freshly cracked black pepper
finely grated Parmesan or pecorino, to serve (optional)

Place the beans in a large pan with a lid and cover with plenty of cold water, at least 15cm above the beans. Bring to the boil, skimming the surface of any white foam. Reduce the heat, partially cover and simmer for 1 hour. Drain the beans.

Wash out the pan, return to the heat and heat half the oil. Add the onion and cook for 10 minutes until just beginning to caramelise. Add the chorizo and cook for another 3 minutes until the sausage starts to release its red spicy flavours and oils, and then stir in the canned tomatoes. Return the half-cooked beans to the pan and cover with plenty of water, at least 7.5cm above the beans. Bring to the boil and then reduce the heat and simmer, partially covered, for another hour until the beans are just tender.

Meanwhile, soak the greens in water to clean them of any dirt and grit. Separate the leaves and shake dry-ish, then cut down to 7.5cm lengths. Add to the pan of just-tender beans and cook for 20 minutes. Taste and season with salt and pepper.

Serve in bowls with plenty of the broth. Sprinkle with a little cheese and drizzle with the remaining oil.

SERVES 6 423 calories, 50.9g carbs, 15.2g fat, 4.2g sat fat, 24g protein

BLACK-EYED PEAS WITH COURGETTES AND SWISS CHARD

This is another firm family favourite. My mother's trick is to add lots of lemon juice towards the end of the cooking time, which not only flavours the peas and broth but also beautifully bleaches the white part of the beans to a clean white colour.

500g dried black-eyed peas, soaked overnight and drained
juice of 3 lemons
750g Swiss chard, washed and cut into 7.5cm lengths
500g courgettes, trimmed, halved and cut into 5cm lengths
sea salt and freshly cracked black pepper
extra virgin olive oil, to serve
anchovies or canned mackerel, to serve (optional)

Place the black-eyed peas in a large pan with a lid and cover with cold water, at least 15cm above the beans. Bring to the boil, skimming the surface of any white foam. Reduce the heat, partially cover and simmer for 1 hour.

Drain the peas, rinse them and then return them to the pan and cover with clean water, this time at least 7.5cm above the peas. Return the pan to the heat and, as soon as the water comes to the boil, add the lemon juice and stir and boil for 5 minutes.

Reduce the heat to a simmer, and season with salt and pepper. Add the Swiss chard and courgettes and cook for a further 30 minutes until the black-eyed peas and vegetables are all tender. Serve warm or at room temperature, drizzled with extra virgin olive oil; if liked, serve with anchovies or canned mackerel.

SERVES 6 299 calories, 50.4g carbs, 1.9g fat, 0.5g sat fat, 23.4g protein

FAVA BEAN STEW

In this dish, the rich, savoury umami flavour that comes from cooking just four ingredients together is satisfying. Everyone I serve this stew to takes a picture of the packet of fava beans, so they can buy them and make it for themselves. My version of this stew differs a little from my mother's. Mum likes to cook the greens from the beginning, I like to add mine halfway through. I also add extra virgin olive oil while the beans are cooking, although my mother does not. However, the result with both is always delicious.

500g cracked dried fava beans
750g Swiss chard (white or multi-coloured, depending on
   the season), washed and cut into 7.5cm lengths
2 splashes of extra virgin olive oil, plus extra to serve
sea salt and freshly cracked black pepper
red wine vinegar, to serve (optional)
canned fish, dressed with olive oil and chopped parsley,
   to serve

Wash the beans, place in a large pan with a lid and cover with plenty of cold water, at least 10cm above the beans. Bring to the boil and skim the surface of any white foam. Reduce the heat, partially cover and simmer for 30 minutes, stirring once or twice.

Add the Swiss chard and extra virgin olive oil, season with salt and pepper and stir well. Partially cover and cook for another 15 minutes until the greens are very tender. Taste for seasoning and adjust if necessary.

Serve in bowls, drizzled with a little more olive oil and a splash of vinegar, if you like. Serve with dressed canned fish.

SERVES 6 237 calories, 30.7g carbs, 3g fat, 0.4g sat fat, 24g protein

Fava Bean Stew (recipe on page 167)

ITALIAN CHICKEN AND LENTIL SOUP

My friend Natalie Poulos, an Australian Italian, married to an Australian Greek, living in New York, makes a similar soup every winter, and I love being invited round for dinner on Monday nights. We then have a very simple lettuce, fennel and cucumber salad – à la Italian – which finishes the meal off to perfection.

1 whole chicken, about 2kg
2 onions, 1 quartered and 1 roughly chopped
3 tablespoons extra virgin olive oil
225g carrots, roughly diced
3 celery sticks, sliced
250g dried Umbrian or small green lentils, washed
3 tablespoons finely chopped dill or flat-leaf parsley,
   plus lemon wedges, to serve
sea salt and freshly cracked black pepper

Place the chicken in a large pan with a lid and fill with enough cold water to cover the chicken completely, with about 20cm extra on top. Bring to the boil and skim the surface of any white foam, then reduce the heat to a simmer. Add the onion quarters, season with salt and pepper and poach, partially covered, for 1 hour until the chicken is very tender. Generally, when the chicken sinks to the bottom, it's a sign that it's cooked. Take the pan off the heat and leave to stand with the lid on for 30 minutes.

Remove the chicken from the pan and set aside. Strain the stock through a fine-mesh sieve, lined with a piece of kitchen paper or muslin, and discard the onion. Reserve the stock. Remove the skin from the chicken and discard. Remove the chicken meat from the carcass and shred into large pieces.

Heat 2 tablespoons of the extra virgin olive oil in a large pan and cook the chopped onion, carrots and celery. Add the lentils and 2 litres of the strained stock, keeping the rest for another time, and bring to the boil. Cover and cook for 30 minutes until the lentils are tender.

Stir in three-quarters of the chicken, season to taste and simmer until the chicken is hot through. Serve scattered with chopped dill or parsley and drizzle over the remaining oil, and the lemon juice. The remaining chicken can be served separately.

SERVES 8 525 calories, 35.5g carbs, 12.1g fat, 2.4g sat fat, 70.9g protein

Italian Chicken and Lentil Soup

Braised Porchetta with Borlotti Beans

BRAISED PORCHETTA WITH BORLOTTI BEANS

Originally, 'porchetta' meant the whole body of the pig, boned, rolled up with rosemary, black pepper and garlic and spit-roasted. However, here I'm taking a bit of poetic licence and using pork belly (no skin for crackling is needed), stuffed with herbs and garlic, and cooking it slowly so that all its flavour infuses the beans. If using freshly podded beans, braise the porchetta first for 1 hour in the stock and then add them to the pot.

500g dried borlotti (or cranberry) beans, soaked
  overnight and drained
1.5kg piece of boned pork belly, with plenty of fat
  trimmed away
2 tablespoons freshly cracked black pepper
6 tablespoons finely chopped rosemary
4 tablespoons finely chopped flat-leaf parsley, plus
  extra to serve
2 garlic cloves, grated on a microplane
finely grated zest of 1 lemon
3 tablespoons extra virgin olive oil
150ml Marsala wine
sea salt and freshly cracked black pepper

Preheat the oven to 160°C/325°F/gas mark 3.

Place the beans in a large oval pan with a lid and fill with enough cold water to cover the beans completely, with about 10cm extra on top. Bring to the boil and skim the surface of any white foam. Reduce to a simmer, partially cover and cook while you prepare the meat.

Open out the pork belly and season all over with salt. In a bowl, combine the black pepper, herbs, garlic and lemon zest. Place the pork, boned-side up, on a clean surface and spread the herb mixture all over. Roll up into a long joint and secure with butcher's string, at 2cm intervals.

Heat 2 tablespoons of the extra virgin olive oil in a large cast-iron pan and sear the meat all over for about 10 minutes, to evenly brown. Remove the meat and add to the pan of beans. Remove all the fat from the cast-iron pan, and gently pour the Marsala wine into the pan; over a low heat, stir into the pan juices to deglaze, then pour this over the meat and beans and season well with salt and extra pepper.

Scrunch up a large piece of parchment paper and wet it with cold water. Open out the paper and lay it directly over the meat. Cover the pan with a tight-fitting lid, place in the oven and braise for 2½ hours until the meat and beans are both very tender.

Remove the meat from the pan and allow it to stand for 5 minutes. Carve it into eight thick slices. Using a slotted spoon, divide the beans between serving bowls or spoon onto a large serving platter and arrange the sliced pork on top. Spoon over some broth, sprinkle with chopped parsley, drizzle with the remaining extra virgin olive oil and serve.

SERVES 8 670 calories, 28.4g carbs, 40.1g fat, 13.4g sat fat, 47.1g protein

CHICKPEAS WITH SPINACH AND PORK SHANKS

This recipe also works very well without the meat. Simply cook the chickpeas on top of the hob and add the spinach during the final 15 minutes of cooking.

500g dried chickpeas, soaked overnight and then drained
2 pork shanks, about 200–300g each
2 tablespoons extra virgin olive oil, plus extra to serve
1 onion, roughly chopped
4 tablespoons finely chopped fresh coriander
4 tablespoons tomato purée
500g spinach (not baby or pousse), washed and trimmed
sea salt and freshly cracked black pepper

Preheat the oven to 160°C/325°F/gas mark 3.

Place the chickpeas in a large pan with a lid and fill with enough cold water to cover the pulses completely, with about 10cm extra on top. Bring to the boil and skim the surface of any white foam. Reduce to a simmer, partially cover and cook while you prepare the rest.

Season the meat and then heat a little of the olive oil in a large cast-iron pan and brown the shanks all over for about 10 minutes. Transfer to a plate lined with kitchen paper.

Drain away all but 2 tablespoons of the meat juices in the pan and sauté the onion for 10 minutes until it begins to caramelise. Stir in the coriander and cook for 2 minutes, then add the tomato purée and cook for a further 3 minutes. Add a ladleful of the chickpea water to the onion mixture and stir until smooth, then pour this into the chickpea pan, stir and season with salt and pepper. Add the pork shanks to the pan.

Scrunch up a large piece of parchment paper and wet it with cold water. Open it out and lay it directly over the meat. Cover the pan with a tight-fitting lid, place in the oven and braise for 2½ hours until the meat falls off the bone and the chickpeas are very tender.

Remove from the hob, add the spinach to the pork and chickpea braise and set aside for the spinach to wilt in the heat of the pan, about 15 minutes. To serve, remove the shanks from the pan and remove the meat from the bones. Discard the bones. Stir the meat into the chickpea stew. Serve in bowls and drizzle with extra virgin olive oil and some black pepper.

SERVES 6 522 calories, 46g carbs, 22.1g fat, 5.4g sat fat, 37.4g protein

Chickpeas with Spinach and Pork Shanks

Slow-roasted Lemon and Garlic Chicken

SLOW-ROASTED LEMON AND GARLIC CHICKEN

This simple garlic and lemon roasted chicken is a classic all over the Mediterranean and my mother makes the very best. She likes to cook it in a deep roasting pan to ensure it slow-roasts to a melting finish. Personally, I like a baking tray with low sides as I find this gives the chicken an even colour. She also often adds Cyprus potatoes halfway through the cooking, and their flavour combines with the lemony pan juices and results in the most perfect roast potatoes. I can't argue with that.

1 whole chicken, about 2kg
3 lemons
6 tablespoons extra virgin olive oil
1 large onion, quartered
2 large rosemary sprigs
4 garlic cloves, peeled, plus 2 whole garlic bulbs, fresh or
    dried, sliced in half
750g starchy potatoes, such as Yukon Gold or Charlotte
sea salt and freshly cracked black pepper

Preheat the oven to 180°C/350°F/gas mark 4. Rub the chicken with salt and pepper.

Squeeze half a lemon into a bowl. Stir in 4 tablespoons olive oil and rub this mix all over the bird, inside and out. Stuff the onion into the cavity with the rosemary, squeezed-out lemon and garlic cloves. Tuck the wing tips under the bird. Tie the legs securely together with butcher's string. Slice the remaining lemons and arrange to cover the base of a roasting pan. Sit the chicken on top and pack the sliced garlic bulbs in around the edges. Pour 100ml water into the pan. Cover the tray with a sheet of parchment paper, then a sheet of foil. Roast for 1¼ hours.

Uncover the chicken and spoon the pan juices over the bird. Add the potatoes, toss in the juices and then return to the oven, uncovered. Roast for a further 1 hour, until the chicken skin is golden brown, the meat is tender and the legs feel very loose. The potatoes should be tender. Divide the chicken into portions and serve with the potatoes and lemony pan juices.

SERVES 6 674 calories, 31.4g carbs, 41.4g fat, 10g sat fat, 45.8g protein

ROASTED STUFFED CHICKEN

Everyone loves a stuffed roast chicken for a wintry weekend meal and almost every country in the Mediterranean has a recipe – they all just have their own version.

1 whole chicken, about 2kg, giblets washed and chopped
stuffing of your choice (see pages 178–179)
3 tablespoons extra virgin olive oil
2 sweet onions, sliced
2 medium carrots, cut in half and chopped into 4cm pieces
3 tablespoons dark sherry or Marsala wine
300ml chicken stock
sea salt and freshly cracked black pepper

Preheat the oven to 200°C/400°F/gas mark 6. Wash the chicken, pat dry with kitchen paper and season well all over. Fill the main cavity with most of the stuffing, reserving a little, and tie the legs together with butcher's string. Fill the front neck cavity with the remaining stuffing and pull the skin down and secure it with a cocktail stick. Rub 2 tablespoons of the olive oil all over the bird, season and tuck the wing tips under the body. Cover the base of a roasting pan with the onions and carrots and drizzle with the remaining oil. Sit the chicken on top, cover the tray with a sheet of parchment paper, followed by a sheet of foil, and roast for 1¾ hours.

Uncover the tray and cook for a further 1 hour to brown the chicken. The legs will move easily when tender. Lift the chicken out of the pan and onto a chopping board, make a tent with parchment paper and foil, and set aside to rest. With a slotted spoon, transfer the onions and carrots to a serving platter.

To make jus, place the roasting pan over a low heat and deglaze with the sherry or Marsala, scraping to release the caramelised flavour stuck to the base. Gradually add the chicken stock and turn up the heat, boiling for 3–4 minutes until the liquid thickens to a light syrup.

Serve the chicken in portions, over the onions and carrots with the stuffing scooped into a bowl on the side; serve the jus ladled on top or in a separate jug.

SERVES 8 665 calories, 22.8g carbs, 45.7g fat, 12.9g sat fat, 41.9g protein

FARRO AND CHESTNUT

75g thick-cut pancetta or bacon, cut into lardons
75g chicken livers, trimmed and cleaned
1 large onion, roughly chopped
150g farro, washed and drained
100g chestnuts, toasted, peeled and chopped
50g chopped mixed herbs, such as flat-leaf parsley,
   sage and thyme

In a sauté pan, cook the pancetta/bacon in its own fat over a low heat until crisp. Set aside. Add the chicken livers to the pan juices, cook for 5 minutes until browned; remove and set aside. Add the onion to the pan juices and cook for 10 minutes until soft and beginning to caramelise. Add the farro with 200ml hot water and simmer for 10 minutes until almost tender. Away from the heat, add the chestnuts, pancetta/bacon and chopped chicken livers. Stir through all the herbs and season to taste. Use to stuff the chicken.

PER 100G 135 calories, 21.3g carbs, 3.4g fat, 1g sat fat, 5.8g protein,

ITALIAN SAUSAGE

200g rustic bread, broken into 2.5cm pieces
50g finely grated Parmesan cheese
4 tablespoons extra virgin olive oil
200g Italian fennel or spicy sausages, casing removed
1 onion, roughly chopped
1 small fennel bulb, trimmed and roughly chopped
4 tablespoons finely chopped flat-leaf parsley
250ml dried mushroom water or chicken stock

Preheat the oven to 200°C/400°F/gas mark 6. Mix the bread on a baking tray with the Parmesan and half the olive oil. Bake until the bread is golden and crunchy. Heat the remaining oil in a large frying pan and brown the sausage meat, breaking it into large clumps. Remove. Add the onion and fennel to the pan juices and sauté to soften, about 8 minutes. In a bowl, mix together all the ingredients and stir in the parsley and stock. Allow to cool and season to taste. Use to stuff the chicken.

PER 100G 147 calories, 9.8g carbs, 10g fat, 3.2g sat fat, 5.5g protein

SPELT, SPINACH AND RICOTTA

2 tablespoons extra virgin olive oil
1 onion, roughly chopped
250g spinach, roughly chopped
100g spelt, partially boiled and drained
½ teaspoon Calabrian chilli flakes (optional)
75g toasted walnuts, chopped
100g fresh ricotta, drained

Heat the olive oil in a large frying pan and cook the onion for 10 minutes until soft and just browned. Add the spinach to the pan and stir-fry until wilted.

Add the spelt and cook for 15 minutes; season to taste and add a little extra oomph with chilli flakes, if you like. Remove from the heat, add the walnuts and parsley and set aside to cool completely. Stir in the ricotta. Use to stuff the chicken.

PER 100G 160 calories, 7.6g carbs, 12.2g fat, 2.2g sat fat, 5g protein

MUSHROOM AND CHESTNUT

15g mixed dried mushrooms
200g rustic bread, torn into 1cm pieces
1 onion, roughly chopped
6 tablespoons fresh thyme leaves
3 tablespoons extra virgin olive oil
100g chestnuts, toasted, peeled and chopped

Preheat the oven to 200°C/400°F/gas mark 6. Place the dried mushrooms in a large bowl and cover with 250ml hot water. Leave to stand for at least 20 minutes. Meanwhile, place the bread on a baking tray and, with your hands, toss with the onion, thyme, olive oil and salt and pepper. Bake for 20 minutes. Remove the soaked mushrooms with a slotted spoon, pat dry with kitchen paper and roughly chop. Add to the bread mixture with the chestnuts. Strain the mushroom water to remove any grit and pour over the bread. Stir into the bread mixture. Use to stuff the chicken.

PER 100G 185 calories, 31.2g carbs, 5g fat, 0.9g sat fat, 5.9g protein

Kleftico (slow-roasted lamb)

KLEFTICO (SLOW-ROASTED LAMB)

The Greek word 'kleftico' translates as 'stolen meat' and refers to days gone by, when poachers would steal a goat or sheep and then cook the pieces very slowly in an underground oven or sealed container, so as not to give themselves away by the cooking aromas! The meat simply cooks in its own juices until it falls off the bone. Serve with a pilaf and a bitter green salad.

2 tablespoons extra virgin olive oil
2 lemons, sliced
2 whole garlic bulbs, cut in half
2.4kg shoulder of lamb
100ml red wine
2 large rosemary sprigs
mixed bitter green salad, to serve
sea salt and freshly cracked black pepper

Preheat the oven to 180°C/350°F/gas mark 4. Cover the base and sides of a deep roasting pan with two really long overlapping pieces of foil, shaped in a big cross. Line each sheet of foil with parchment paper and drizzle the base with a tiny bit of the oil. Arrange the lemon slices and garlic on top.

Rub the lamb all over with a little oil and a good amount of salt and pepper. Place on top of the lemons and garlic. Drizzle over the red wine and top with the rosemary. Wrap the parchment and then the foil over the meat and seal the parcel well by folding and scrunching over the ends to seal.

Transfer the roasting pan to the oven and roast for 3 hours, until the meat is falling off the bone. Open up the foil and paper and return to the oven for another 30 minutes for the meat to brown a little.

Use a spoon and fork to lift the meat gently from the bone, and serve over the green salad, adding a few roasted garlic cloves and lemon slices to each portion.

SERVES 8 611 calories, 2.2g carbs, 46.7g fat, 20.8g sat fat, 43.3g protein

LEG OF LAMB WITH ANCHOVIES AND OREGANO

Roasted lamb, stuffed with salt-cured anchovies and dried oregano, is very hard to beat. This version cooks the lamb to medium-rare but, if you prefer, add on an extra 2 hours of cooking time, keeping the meat covered, to achieve meat that falls off the bone, like the Kleftico on this page.

2.4kg boned leg of lamb
1 large onion, sliced

FOR THE ANCHOVY RUB
8 salt-cured anchovies, filleted (see page 34) and
  finely chopped
2 tablespoons dried oregano
2 tablespoons finely chopped rosemary
2 tablespoons extra virgin olive oil
2 teaspoons Calabrian chilli flakes (optional)
sea salt and freshly cracked black pepper

Preheat the oven to 220°C/425°F/gas mark 7. In a bowl, mix all the anchovy rub ingredients together.

Open out the leg of lamb and rub all over with the anchovy mixture. Roll the meat back up again and secure with butcher's string at 2cm intervals.

Arrange the onion slices in a roasting pan and place the lamb on top. Pour in about 100ml water and roast for 20 minutes until the meat takes on some colour. Reduce the oven temperature to 190°C/375°F/gas mark 5 and roast for a further 1 hour (10 minutes per 500g) for medium rare. If you prefer lamb 'medium', cook for 15 minutes per 500g. Add extra water to the roasting pan if you find it's drying up.

Remove from the oven and pour the pan juices into a bowl. Allow the joint to rest for 15–20 minutes. Chill the meat juices, for the fat to rise to the top then skim to remove the fat. Heat the meat juices with a little more water (about 100ml).

Thinly carve the lamb and serve with the meat juices spooned over. Serve with roasted or grilled vegetables on the side.

SERVES 8 623 calories, 1.8g carbs, 41.6g fat, 17.3g sat fat, 60.4g protein

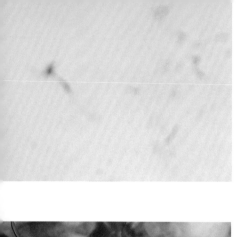

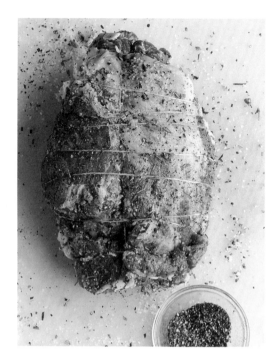

Left: olives growing; bottom left: salt-cured anchovies; top centre: prepared leg of lamb with anchovies, oregano and pepper; top right: dried oregano; below: sheep grazing in an orchard.

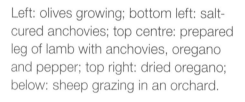

Roasted Leg of Lamb with Anchovies and Oregano (recipe on page 181)

BRAISED OCTOPUS TO BE CHAR-GRILLED

There are many theories regarding the best method for this, but the following has given me the best results. You can then choose how to serve the braised octopus. I love to char-grill mine over a charcoal barbecue and serve with one of the sauces on pages 96–99. Or you can simply serve it drizzled with extra virgin olive oil and chopped parsley. And don't throw away the poaching or braising liquid as it beautifully flavours a risotto or pilaf.

4 tablespoons extra virgin olive oil
1 onion, quartered
3 garlic cloves, bashed to split the skins
15g thyme sprigs
1.5kg octopus (either 1 large or several small)
sea salt
chopped parsley, lemon juice and extra virgin olive oil,
 to serve (optional)

Preheat the oven to 180°C/350°F/gas mark 4. Heat the olive oil in a large braising pan with a lid and cook the onion, garlic and thyme until the onion caramelises a little. Remove from the heat.

Bring a large stockpot of salted water to the boil and scald the octopus by dipping it in the boiling water three times over. (Each time, hold the octopus with tongs and plunge for 10 seconds and then lift out again.) Transfer to the braising pan and pour in enough of the scalding water to cover the octopus. Cover with a large piece of dampened parchment paper, followed by the lid and transfer to the oven. Braise for 1½–2 hours. If using several small octopi, you will only need to cook for 45 minutes.

Leave the octopus to cool in the pan for 30 minutes and then lift out of the liquid and transfer to a chopping board. Use a sharp knife to cut into 10–15cm pieces. Grill or dress with parsley, lemon juice and extra virgin olive oil to serve.

SERVES 6 287 calories, 2.8g carbs, 10.7g fat, 1.8g sat fat, 45.3g protein

RED WINE-BRAISED OCTOPUS

Serve as a starter or as part of a mezze or tapas meal. Or in wintertime, serve over a bulgur wheat pilaf (page 58).

3 tablespoons extra virgin olive oil
2 large onions, roughly chopped
3 garlic cloves, bashed to split the skins
2 tablespoons coriander seeds, lightly crushed
500ml full-bodied red wine
3 bay leaves
2kg octopus, or several smaller ones to make up the weight

FOR THE SALAD
2 shallots, thinly sliced on a mandolin
3 tablespoons red wine vinegar
2 teaspoons toasted coriander seeds, lightly crushed
25g flat-leaf parsley, separated into small sprigs
6 tablespoons extra virgin olive oil

Preheat the oven to 180°C/350°F/gas mark 4. Heat the oil in a large braising pot, add the onions, garlic and coriander seeds and sauté until the onions just start to brown. Add the red wine and bay leaves and bring to the boil.

Meanwhile, bring a large stockpot of salted water to the boil and scald the octopus by dipping it in the boiling water three times over. (Each time, hold the octopus with tongs and plunge for 10 seconds and then lift out.) Transfer to the braising pot and cover with a large piece of dampened parchment paper. Cover and braise in the oven for 2 hours until tender. (If using several small octopi, cook for 45 minutes only.) Remove from the heat and cool for 30 minutes in the covered pot.

Place the shallot in a bowl with the vinegar and coriander seeds. Leave to stand for 10 minutes. Remove the shallots and mix with the parsley. Reserve the vinegar.

Transfer the octopus to a chopping board and slice into 7.5cm pieces. Gently toss the octopus with the parsley salad. Add the olive oil to the reserved vinegar, taste and season. Drizzle over the octopus salad and serve.

SERVES 6 515 calories, 5.3g carbs, 21.4g fat, 3.4g sat fat, 61.1g protein

Red Wine-braised Octopus

Confit of Swordfish

CONFIT OF SWORDFISH

Swordfish can sometimes be a little dry and disappointing and yet this way of cooking it delivers the most deliciously moist results. I also like to cook thick tuna, salmon and cod steaks in the same way and serve them with Caper and Olive Salsa (see page 97).

It is easy to store confit of fish – allow the fish and oil to cool separately. Remove the flavourings from the oil and combine the fish and oil again in a glass or plastic re-sealable container so that the fish is completely submerged (add a little more oil if necessary). Keep in the fridge for up to 3 days and serve at room temperature with a salad.

500ml extra virgin olive oil
2 garlic cloves, bashed to split the skins
½ teaspoon Calabrian chilli flakes (optional)
2 rosemary sprigs (or flat-leaf parsley, thyme or marjoram)
4 swordfish steaks, 150g each and about 2cm thick, skin removed
1–2 tablespoons sea salt flakes

FOR THE SALAD
225g sugar snap peas, trimmed
225g fat asparagus tips
extra virgin olive oil
100g pea or broad bean tendrils
100g watercress
juice of 1 lemon or 3 tablespoons red wine vinegar

Place the oil in a large, deep saucepan and heat with the garlic, chilli flakes (if using) and herbs to 52°C/125°F. Remove from the heat and allow to stand for 30 minutes for the flavours to infuse the oil.

Meanwhile, rub the fish all over with the salt flakes and set aside for 30 minutes at room temperature to flavour and cure slightly. Rinse in cold water and pat dry with kitchen paper.

Return the oil to the heat, gently bring up to 60°C/140°F and add the fish, then take off the heat and allow to sit for 10–15 minutes; return the pan to the heat to return its temperature to 60°C/140°F throughout the cooking period for the fish.

Lift out a piece of fish and press gently between your fingertips – it should still be springy. Salmon and tuna should have changed colour slightly and white fish should have turned opaque. Drain the fish and place on a large platter.

For the salad, place a grill pan or cast-iron frying pan over a high heat. Add the sugar snap peas and asparagus with a drop or two of extra virgin olive oil and sear for 1–2 minutes, blackening them here and there in places.

Transfer the peas and asparagus to a bowl, add the pea or broad bean tendrils and watercress and dress with lemon juice or vinegar. Toss to combine. Divide the salad between four serving plates, add the fish and serve with a little more dressing or Caper and Olive Salsa (see page 97).

SERVES 4
CONFIT 728 calories, 0.5g carbs, 68.1g fat, 10.3g sat fat, 27.2g protein
SALAD 58 calories, 4.2g carbs, 2.4g fat, 0.4g sat fat, 5.1g protein

Index

Footnotes

Bach-Faig, A., Berry, E.M., Lairon, D., Reguant, J., et al., (2011). Mediterranean diet pyramid today. Science and cultural updates. *Public Health Nutrition*;14(12A): 2274–84.

De Lorgeril, M., Salen, P., Martin J.L., Monjaud, I., Delaye, J., Mamelle, N., (1999). Mediterranean diet, traditional risk factors, and the rate of cardiovascular complications after myocardial infarction: final report of the Lyon Diet Heart Study. *Circulation*; 16(99): 779–85.

Estruch, R., Ros, E., Salas-Salvado, J., Covas, M.I., et al., (2013). Primary prevention of cardiovascular disease with a Mediterranean diet. *N Engl J Med*; 368(14): 1279–90.

Georgoulis, M., Kontogianni, M.D., Yiannakouris, N., (2014). Mediterranean diet and diabetes: prevention and treatment. *Nutrients*; 6: 1406–23.

Lasa A., Miranda, J., Bullo, M., Casas, R., et al., (2014). Comparative effect of two Mediterranean diets versus a low-fat diet on glycaemic control in individuals with type 2 diabetes. *European Journal of Clinical Nutrition*; 68: 767–72.

Mente, A., de Koning, L., Shannon, H.S., Anand, S.S., (2009). A systematic review of the evidence supporting a causal link between dietary factors and coronary heart disease. *Arch Intern Med*; 169(7): 659–69.

Shai, I., Schwarzfuchs, D., Henkin, Y., Shahar, D., et al., (2008). Weight loss with a low-carbohydrate, Mediterranean, or low-fat diet. *N Engl J Med*; 359(3): 229–41.

Sofi, F., Cesari, F., Abbate, R., Gensini, G.F., Casini, A., (2008). Adherence to Mediterranean diet and health status: meta-analysis. *BMJ*; 337: a1344.

Trichopoulou, A., Lagiou, P., Kuper, H., Trichopoulou, D., (2000). Cancer and Mediterranean dietary traditions. Review. *Cancer Epidemiology Biomarkers & Prevention*; 9: 869–73.

Trichopoulou, A., Vasilopoulou, E., (2000). Mediterranean diet and longevity. *British Journal of Nutrition*; 84(2): 205–9.

Metric / Imperial Conversion Charts

Glossary for the US

Weight conversions		Linear conversions		Volume conversions	
5 g	⅛ oz	2 mm	¹⁄₁₆ in	1.25 ml	¼ tsp
10 g	¼ oz	3 mm	⅛ in	2.5 ml	½ tsp
15 g	½ oz	5 mm	¼ in	5 ml	1 tsp
25/30g	1 oz	8 mm	3/8 in	10 ml	2 tsp
35 g	1¼ oz	10 mm / 1 cm	½ in	15 ml	1 tbsp / 3 tsp / ½ fl oz
40 g	1½ oz	15 mm	⅝ in	30 ml	2 tbsp / 1 fl oz
50 g	1¾ oz	2 cm	¾ in	45 ml	3 tbsp
55 g	2 oz	2.5 cm	1 in	50 ml	2 fl oz
60 g	2¼ oz	3 cm	1¼ in	60 ml	4 tbsp
70 g	2½ oz	4 cm	1½ in	75 ml	5 tbsp / 2½ fl oz
85 g	3 oz	4.5 cm	1¾ in	90 ml	6 tbsp
90 g	3¼ oz	5 cm	2 in	100 ml	3½ fl oz
100 g	3½ oz	5.5 cm	2¼ in	125 ml	4 fl oz
115 g	4 oz	6 cm	2½ in	150 ml	5 fl oz / ¼ pt
125 g	4½ oz	7 cm	2¾ in	175 ml	6 fl oz
140 g	5 oz	8 cm	3¼ in	200 ml	7 fl oz / 1/3 pt
150 g	5½ oz	9 cm	3½ in	225 ml	8 fl oz
175 g	6 oz	9.5 cm	3¾ in	250 ml	9 fl oz
200 g	7 oz	10 cm	4 in	300 ml	10 fl oz / ½ pt
225 g	8 oz	11 cm	4¼ in	350 ml	12 fl oz
250 g	9 oz	12 cm	4½ in	400 ml	14 fl oz
275 g	9¾ oz	13 cm	5 in	425 ml	15 fl oz / ¾ pt
280 g	10 oz	14 cm	5½ in	450 ml	16 fl oz
300 g	10½ oz	15 cm	6 in	500 ml	18 fl oz
325 g	11½ oz	16 cm	6¼ in	568 ml	1 pint
350 g	12 oz	17 cm	6½ in	600 ml	20 fl oz
375 g	13 oz	18 cm	7 in	700 ml	1¼ pint
400 g	14 oz	19 cm	7½ in	850 ml	1½ pint
425 g	15 oz	20 cm	8 in	1 litre	1¾ pint
450 g	1 lb	22 cm	8½ in	1.2 litres	2 pints
500 g	1 lb 2 oz	23 cm	9 in	1.3 litres	2¼ pints
550 g	1 lb 4 oz	24 cm	9½ in	1.4 litres	2½ pints
600 g	1 lb 5 oz	25 cm	10 in	1.7 litres	3 pints
650 g	1 lb 7 oz	26 cm	10½ in	2 litres	3½ pints
700 g	1 lb 9 oz	27 cm	10¾ in	2.5 litres	4½ pints
750 g	1 lb 10 oz	28 cm	11 in	2.8 litres	5 pints
800 g	1 lb 12 oz	29 cm	11½ in	3 litres	5¼ pints
850 g	1 lb 14 oz	30 cm	12 in		
900 g	2 lb				
950 g	2 lb 2 oz				
1 kg	2 lb 4 oz				
1.25 kg	2 lb 12 oz				
z1.5 kg	3 lb 5 oz				
1.6 kg	3 lb 8 oz				
1.8 kg	4 lb				
2 kg	4 lb 8 oz				
2.4 kg	5 lb 4 oz				

Aubergine – eggplant

Barbecue – grill

Beetroot – beet

Borlotti beans – cranberry beans

Broad bean – fava bean

Chicory – endive

Chilli flakes – red pepper flakes

Coriander (fresh) – cilantro

Coriander (dried) – coriander

Courgette – zucchini

Frying pan – skillet

Grill – broil/broiler

Heritage tomatoes – heirloom tomatoes

Kitchen paper – paper towels

Lebanese cucumbers – Persian cucumbers

Minced pork or lamb – ground pork or lamb

Muslin – cheesecloth

Parchment paper – wax paper

Pea shoots – pea tendrils

Peppers – bell peppers

Prawn – shrimp

Pulses – legumes

Rocket – arugula

Spring onions – scallions

Starter – appertizer

Tomato purée – tomato paste